Stubby THE

The True Story o

War Dog

World War I's Bravest Dog

ANN BAUSUM

SIBERT HONOR AWARD–WINNING AUTHOR

NATIONAL GEOGRAPHIC

WASHINGTON, D.C.

Economy France.
March 1919.

This one is for the dogs—
and for the people who have
loved them, especially
J. Robert Conroy.
—A.B.

Contents

6 **Foreword**

8 **Introduction**

10 **CHAPTER ❶ A Dog's Best Friend**

18 **CHAPTER ❷ Over There**

28 **CHAPTER ❸ In the Trenches**

40 **CHAPTER ❹ Victory Lap**

48 **CHAPTER ❺ At Ease, Sgt. Stubby**

56 **Afterword**

62 **Time Line**

64 **Research Notes**

65 **Acknowledgments**

66 **Bibliography**

68 **Resource Guide**

69 **Citations**

70 **Index**

71 **Illustrations Credits**

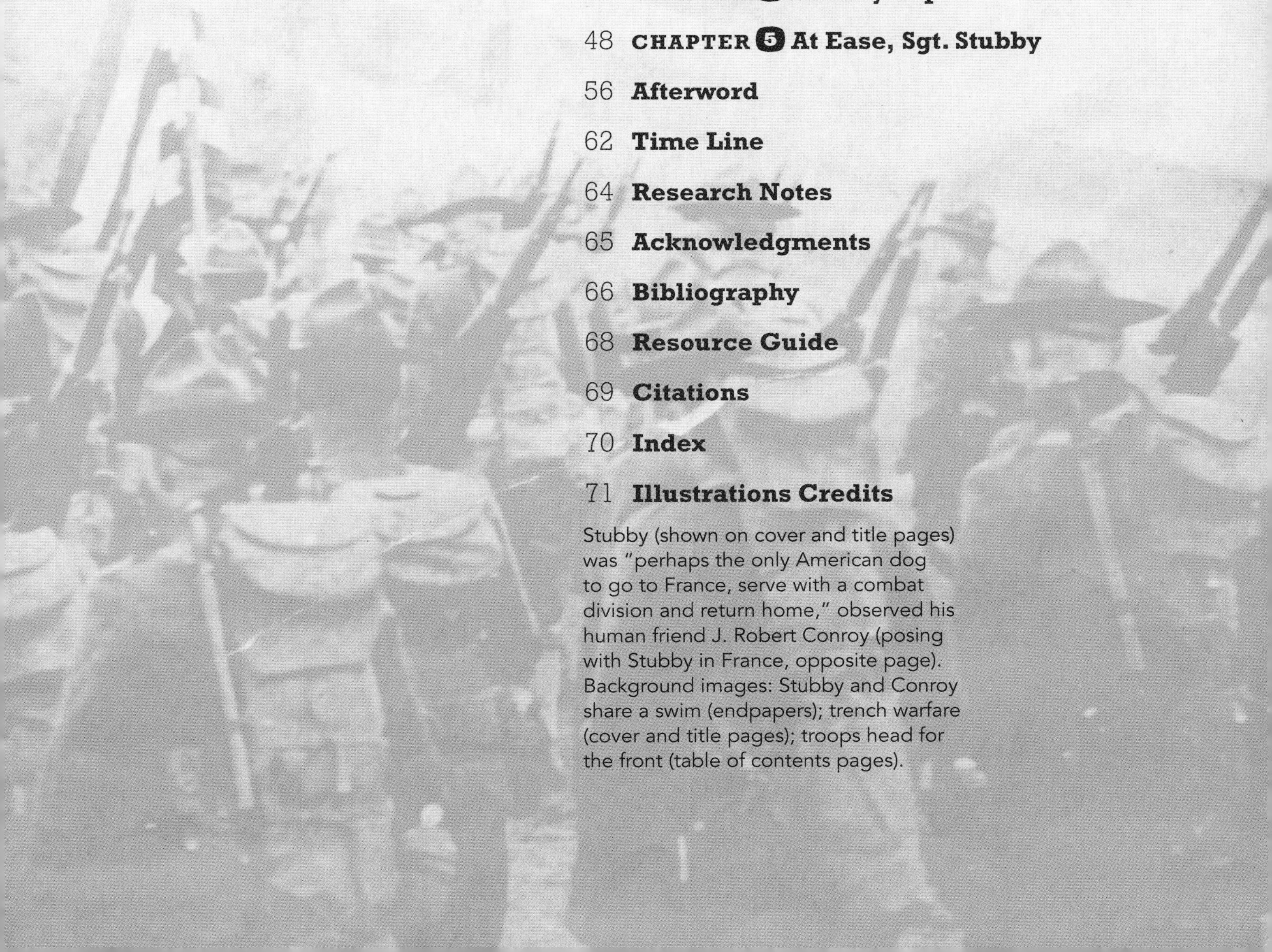

Stubby (shown on cover and title pages)
was "perhaps the only American dog
to go to France, serve with a combat
division and return home," observed his
human friend J. Robert Conroy (posing
with Stubby in France, opposite page).
Background images: Stubby and Conroy
share a swim (endpapers); trench warfare
(cover and title pages); troops head for
the front (table of contents pages).

Foreword

I was always told by my father and my grandfather, J. Robert Conroy, that we were "raised by dogs." Dogs were an important part of my family, always found in the homes of relatives on both sides, and, later, in my own home, too.

As a child, I didn't really understand what my father and grandfather had meant. After all, you have to teach dogs to obey you and not chew up your shoes. We raise *them*, not the other way around.

But as I grew older, I came to understand what they meant through the stories my grandfather told me about the pride and joy of his life: his beloved dog, Stubby.

Stubby was more than a pet. He and my grandfather were truly life partners. They had faced the dangers of a war in a foreign country together, and they shared a special bond.

A war zone is a treacherous environment. It is noisy and chaotic, with danger lurking at every turn: incoming enemy fire, poison gas, and the enemy soldiers themselves. There is never a peaceful moment.

Yet Stubby was able to bring a sense of calm and comfort to his soldiers, his team.

His hypersensitive sense of smell allowed him to warn his soldiers of incoming gas.

His acute sense of hearing allowed him to track the enemy.

His warmth and loyalty allowed him to stand by his wounded comrades and provide assurance that help would arrive.

J. Robert Conroy (second from right) and Stubby gathered with friends in Washington, D.C., for a commemorative snapshot.

Ann Bausum has captured Stubby's unique dedication and his bond, not only with my grandfather, but with all the troops in the 102nd Regiment. She has captured Stubby's noble service to our country at a time of great need, too.

Through my grandfather and his dog, Stubby, I learned that being raised by dogs meant learning the meaning of unconditional love, being both trustworthy and faithful, living with dignity and without hesitation or regret, and caring for others less fortunate or in need.

My grandfather returned Stubby's steadfast love and devotion in kind, and he made certain his friend always had the best care, even to his death in my grandfather's arms.

My grandfather was never able to let go of the wartime memories, both good and bad, that he and Stubby had shared. His deep-seated attachment and respect for Stubby lasted a lifetime: He never raised—or was raised by—another dog again.

—Curtis Deane

Introduction

This much we know for sure: There was a war. There was a soldier. And there was a dog.

I discovered the dog by accident in 2010, when I was researching *Unraveling Freedom,* my book about the American home front during World War I. The animal's story seemed so incredible that at first I did not believe it could be true. How could one dog have been so capable, survived so many battles, gained such fame? Surely someone had made him up.

But the story was true, at least large parts of it, and it grabbed hold of me in the way good stories do: with a smile, coming to mind unexpectedly, and showing up with growing frequency. Doggedly, one could say. Two years later my publisher asked me to invent three nonfiction book ideas to share at a party, two fake and one true. I trotted out Stubby as part of the mix. And that's how this book came into being, as a strategic joke at a gathering of librarians and publishers. I think Stubby would have liked that twist, or at least J. Robert Conroy would have, as the devoted keeper of Stubby and his fame.

Some people might say that I am an unlikely candidate to write a book about a dog. For one thing, all of my other titles have focused on the more serious sides of history. Plus, full disclosure, I haven't owned a dog in 40 years. All of the dogs from my childhood met tragic ends. Pooh the cocker spaniel, hit by a car. Benet the Chihuahua, disappeared. Checkers the Dalmatian, hit by the mail truck. Checkers II, another Dalmatian, put to sleep due to illness. Truth be told, in the decades since, I'd lost interest in dogs. My heart belonged to cats and cats alone.

As I began to research the life of Stubby, I rather thought my lack of affection for dogs might add objectivity to my work. But I would be dishonest to maintain this claim. Instead, Stubby charmed me just as he had charmed the guests at that party and almost everyone he ever met. Halfway through my research I found myself checking

The first dog I knew was a cocker spaniel my brother had named Pooh, in honor of Winnie the Pooh (above, the author, age two, with her brother David). Everyone loved Pooh!

books out of the library that were totally unrelated to my project. How to choose a dog, profiles for different breeds of dogs, how to care for a dog, and so on. For no rational reason, I, the ignorer of dogs, began to think about acquiring one. That is the spell of Stubby.

This enchanting creature left behind a tantalizing trail of historical evidence that includes random sources, misinformation, and solid fact. One of the many stops I made as I navigated that path was the storage area for the Smithsonian Institution's National Museum of American History. I wanted to see a jacket that Stubby had worn, and a thoughtful curator indulged me. The garment is stored in a flat box with a protective sunken center. Even now it gives off faint smells, a sort of custom blending of leather and dog and U.S. Army and history.

Follow your noses, readers, and turn the pages of this book. Meet this dog. He was just a stray dog, a dog adopted by an American soldier. A dog who went on to become the most famous dog of the Great War, the War to End All Wars, World War I. A brave dog. A loyal dog. A lovable dog.

Here is his story.

"The one absolutely unselfish friend that a man can have in this selfish world, the one that never deserts him, the one that never proves ungrateful or treacherous, is his dog."

—George G. Vest, speaking as the attorney for a lawsuit involving a dead dog, September 23, 1870, Warrensburg, Missouri

A DOG'S BEST FRIEND

The dog came out of nowhere.

No one knows the details of his breeding or birth. No one knows whether he had looked on anyone else as master, how long he'd wandered without a home, whether he was lost or abandoned. No one knows whether he'd ever had another name.

His closest relatives appeared to be Boston terriers—or, as they were once called, Boston bull terriers. The dog's coat was brindle patterned, a sandy brown streaked with waves of darker fur. He was a handsome enough dog—muscular, wiry, solid—standing not quite two feet tall, on all fours, and measuring a bit more than two feet long from snout to stubby tail. White patches highlighted his chest and face, emphasizing his dark nose and eyes. White fur capped his front feet, too, and it lightly frosted his back paws.

The story goes that the stray dog with a stub of a tail already lived around the

J. Robert Conroy and a stray dog named Stubby met on the athletic fields of Yale University (above, student recruits train in the Yale Bowl). Their friendship endured on battlefields and beyond (left page).

athletic stadium of Yale University in the spring of 1917. If he didn't, it wouldn't have taken him long to figure out that he should. That same spring the United States had joined the fight that would become known as World War I, and by summertime members of the Connecticut National Guard had started training on Yale's athletic grounds. It took

a lot of food to feed a camp full of active men, and that meant a lot of cooking went on, day after day. And *that* meant stray dogs could enjoy an endless source of bones and scraps and scrounging.

It's likely that the dog the soldiers nicknamed "Stubby" was not the only stray that lived off the leavings of the men's meals. He does seem to have been among the most likeable, though, and he was clearly exceptionally clever. Before long the mysterious drifter had become a spunky pal for the service members, a friend who could be counted on to visit camp tents, trot along for military training exercises, and memorize the locations of the mess kitchens.

At some point during the endless weeks of summer training the dog chose a master. He continued to roam the grassy grid of camp "streets," visiting favorite soldiers and feeding posts. But Stubby took a special liking to James Robert Conroy, a 25-year-old enlisted man from New Britain, Connecticut, and Conroy clearly took a shine to Stubby. In the following months, they bonded until, by fall, they were almost inseparable.

Conroy, just like Stubby, was short on family. His father had died when Conroy was seven years old, and at age 21 he'd lost his mother, too. His siblings—two older sisters, one younger brother, and the two youngest children, twin girls—had regrouped after their mother's death and begun a lifelong tradition of caring for one another. Looking after a friendly dog suited Conroy's nature. Hanging around a kind human suited Stubby's.

The two teamed up to support a war that had begun three years earlier in Europe. Fighting had broken out within weeks of the murder of the heir to the Austro-Hungarian Empire in late June of 1914. By fall Europe and neighboring countries had split into opposing forces.

Conroy served in the Yankee Division with the headquarters company (above) for the 102nd Infantry, one of its four regiments of foot soldiers. Stubby became the group's mascot.

The Central Powers of Germany, Austria-Hungary, and eventually Turkey squared off against the Allied Powers of France, Great Britain, Russia, and later Italy.

The resulting battles brought together an odd blending of new technologies with old-fashioned military strategy. Fully automated machine guns fired on cloth-covered foot soldiers. Armored tanks crossed battlefields along with horse-riding officers. Silent submarines sneaked up on lumbering supply ships. Combat planes shared air space with messenger pigeons. Cannons—renamed artillery guns—lobbed shells the size of humans toward opposing soldiers stationed miles away, out of sight and sound.

This mismatch of equipment and strategy led to the invention of a new way of fighting: trench warfare. Soldiers dug bunkers and trenches so they could hide below ground from artillery and machine-gun fire. They created miles and miles of trenches, in fact—trenches that became, by default, borders of their own. The "No Man's Land" between them offered the likelihood of death to many of the soldiers who entered it, and millions perished, sometimes by the hundreds of thousands at a single battlefront. By 1917 the warring armies were at a stalemate, so dug in that neither side could dislodge the other. In an effort to starve out its opponent, Germany began attacking noncombat supply ships, including ones from America. This added aggression helped draw the United States into the war on April 6, 1917. Robert Conroy volunteered for the cause six weeks later.

Conroy was one of some 3,000 residents from his hometown who joined the war effort. Many, like Conroy, signed up for duty voluntarily, but plenty of others were conscripted, or required to participate. The nation's fighting forces reflected its diversity as a land of immigrants. The rolls of soldiers from New Britain, Connecticut, stretched from John Abate, born in Italy, to Joseph Zysek, a native of Russia. Others hailed from such countries as Poland, Persia (now Iran), Greece, and Armenia. For reasons about as obscure as Stubby's origins, Conroy and the other infantrymen, or foot soldiers of World War I, came to be known as doughboys.

Stubby charmed Conroy and the other doughboys stationed in New Haven, Connecticut. He was by all accounts a wonderful dog—cheerful, faithful, friendly, lovable. He formed an intense loyalty to men in uniform, at least men wearing a U.S. military uniform. While the soldiers trained, Stubby studied the scene. He learned the meanings of the various bugle calls that set the pace of the day, from morning reveille to evening taps. The most anticipated call, at least for Stubby, became the mess call, or the call to eat, which of course sounded multiple times a day. The dog learned how to march in formation, too, responding to the same commands that guided the men as they paraded on the athletic fields of Yale University. In short, Stubby learned how to be a perfectly good soldier, albeit one with four legs.

Stubby mastered another military maneuver, too: the salute. It's likely that Conroy taught the dog this mandatory military hand signal of greeting and respect. To salute, Stubby would sit down, rear up from his front legs, raise his right paw to the right side of his face, and gaze seriously at his counterpart until his gesture of respect had been answered. Hearts inevitably melted. By the time Stubby had "completed his boot training," as Conroy put it, he had become the "full-fledged mascot" for Conroy's unit.

In some ways, Stubby's training was more complete than that of his fellow doughboys. The U.S. Army struggled as it sought to swell its ranks from thousands of men to millions. Factories rushed to catch up with demand, and soldiers were lucky to train with even out-of-date rifles. The men balanced the lack of practical drills with extra physical training. They exercised with jumping jacks, practiced push-ups, and marched endlessly. Such activities built endurance and strength in the men, especially as they marched day in and day out, sometimes hauling heavy backpacks.

Week after week Stubby hiked along with the men by day, visited the soldiers in their tents at night, and rose to the next dawn's call of reveille, punctuated with regular trips to the camp kitchens. And so things might have continued forever, as far as Stubby was concerned, except for one huge problem, totally unknowable within the live-in-the-moment world of a dog: There was a war

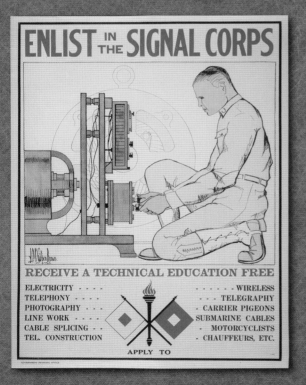
The government recruited soldiers with promises of education (left) and adventure, but training started with the basics (above, digging trenches). The services included African Americans, concentrated into all-black units (below), and women working as nurses in an era before females participated in combat.

Simulated combat (above and right) was part of the soldiers' training on both sides of the Atlantic. When the men reached France, they traveled in forty and eight boxcars (below), designed to haul 40 men (hommes) or 8 horses (chevaux).

Marines ride in forty and eight boxcars toward their French training camp.

to fight. Thoughts of war and eventual departure must have grown among the men at Stubby's camp, and the dog may well have sensed that change was afoot.

That change hit at the end of the summer when Conroy's regiment struck its tents and loaded its backpacks. Then, after nightfall, the men began to leave their temporary home on the Yale athletic fields, bound via train for the port city of Newport News, Virginia. Conroy later wrote that "Stubby was sadly told it was useless to go any farther because dogs would not be permitted to board the ship." Conroy added, with his trademark sense of humor: "Stubby naturally could not understand

that." But Stubby could see that his endless supply of free bones was on the move, not to mention his best friend. Under the cover of darkness, Stubby followed the soldiers to the train depot and hopped aboard the railroad car. No one tried to stop him.

Conroy wasn't one to break rules, but, after reaching Virginia, his fondness for Stubby led him to hatch a plan. Conroy recruited the help of a sympathetic crew member from their Europe-bound ship. With his help, the plan just might work. Thus it was that in the fall of 1917, as Conroy and his fellow soldiers prepared to march on board the *Minnesota*, his accomplice, the seaman, wrapped Stubby inside a blanket, urged the dog to be quiet, and, with the animal hidden in his arms, climbed the gangplank onto the ship.

2

"Over there, over there,
Send the word, send the word over there—
That the Yanks are coming,
The Yanks are coming . . .
And we won't come back 'til it's over
over there."

—Lines from the chorus of "Over There," composed by George M. Cohan, 1917

OVER THERE

Almost immediately after stepping onto the *Minnesota*, Stubby's smuggler hustled him below decks. Then he hid his stowaway inside a coal bin in the ship's vast engine room. After the vessel was well out to sea, Robert Conroy and his accomplice brought Stubby out of hiding. No one seemed to mind. Seasickness bothered plenty of the ship's passengers, including cavalry horses penned within the vessel. But not Stubby. During their multi-week journey, the dog frolicked on the decks with Conroy and other doughboys, consumed food scraps offered by the ship's cook, and kept sentries company as they watched for enemy submarines. He was on hand as off-duty soldiers wrote letters home, read, and dealt out endless hands of cards, too.

When the *Minnesota* reached the French port of St. Nazaire, Conroy hid Stubby inside a blanket and carried him off the ship while some friends distracted any watchful eyes with what Conroy called "good interference." No one could have expected the dog's presence to remain a secret from authorities forever, though, and indeed it did not. The story goes that Conroy's commanding officer soon spotted the animal. Before the man could determine some sort of consequence, however, Stubby sat down on his haunches, reared back from his front

The U.S. government promoted the duty, glory, and adventure of wartime service (left), but few men enjoyed the troop ship journey over and back (above, the *Minnesota*).

feet, raised his right paw, and saluted him. Seemingly that trick erased all thoughts of punishment, either for man or beast, and the dog was allowed to stay with Conroy's unit as its mascot.

Conroy and Stubby served with the headquarters company for the 102nd Infantry, one of four regiments of foot soldiers within the 26th Division. Because most of the members of the 26th came from New England states, these troops were nicknamed the Yankee Division. Conroy and his fellow soldiers were among the first American fighting forces to reach France, and they continued their training in Europe while they waited for other divisions to reach the war zone. The commander for the 28,000 men of the Yankee Division was the popular Maj. Gen. Clarence Edwards. His soldiers "would do anything for him," observed military historian Edward G. Lengel.

Conroy worked in the intelligence section of the 102nd's headquarters company, and his unit managed military information for the regiment of 3,700 or so men. When Conroy was dispatched to carry messages to other outfits, Stubby trotted alongside the soldier's horse. When Conroy stood guard, so did Stubby. When Conroy's turns came for a furlough, or break from duty, Stubby took a break with him. Early on, for example, the pair toured the rolling countryside of eastern France, visiting the birthplace of Joan of Arc and other landmarks.

All that marching practice came in handy when troops moved between battlefields at the war front. Soldiers from the 101st Infantry of Robert Conroy's Yankee Division marched through Soulosse, France, with their ammunition train (above) under the curious gaze of local children.

n January of 1918 Col. John Henry Parker became the commander of Conroy's regiment. This seasoned veteran of other American wars had earned the nickname "Machine Gun" Parker because of his expertise in the use of these rapid-firing weapons. Parker knew Stubby because Conroy served in the colonel's headquarters company. It was later reported that "Stubby was the only member of his regiment that could talk back to him and get away with it." When it came time for the 102nd to head to battle, Machine Gun Parker ordered Stubby to go, too. Now Stubby was the mascot for Conroy's entire regiment, not just its headquarters company.

On February 5, 1918, the Yankee Division reached the front lines. The soldiers manned positions in northeastern France at a battlefront named for a local highway, Chemin des Dames, or the Ladies Road. The Germans held fortified positions to the east while the French maintained their own defenses opposite them. If the Germans broke through this barrier, they might have been able to capture the French capital of Paris, some 60 miles to the southwest. It was the Americans' job to make sure that didn't happen.

"**Stubby was always on his own—he** was never tied up anywhere," explained Conroy. During combat "he seemed to know that no one could bother with him," Conroy added, "and that he had to stay quietly under cover if he expected to remain a live mascot." Everyone in the Yankee Division who met Stubby liked him, from the division commander on down. To Conroy he was, simply, his "closest comrade . . . during the war."

Conroy's duties on the war front varied. Sometimes he assisted the commanding officers of his headquarters; at other times he took his place, rifle at the ready, beside the soldiers in the French network of trenches and dugouts. Mostly Stubby stuck by Conroy, but sometimes he sought out sleeping soldiers, cuddled up to them, and kept watch. On other occasions he joined sentries at their guard posts.

On several occasions Stubby disappeared during battles. No doubt Conroy worried about his friend, but later on he would joke that Stubby had gone AWOL, short for Absent Without Leave. Stubby always returned eventually, although on one occasion he apparently needed some extra help getting "home." The story goes that a French soldier found Stubby during one of his rambles and adopted him. Sometime later a doughboy from the Yankee Division spotted the man leading Stubby on a leash. The American reportedly ordered the Frenchman to surrender his new pet and refused to leave until he did. Then the rescuer returned the mascot to his unit.

Although smuggling a dog over to Europe was somewhat unusual, finding one on the front lines was not. All of the European countries, Allied and enemy, maintained a force of trained dogs. These animals numbered in the thousands on both sides, and they did a little bit of everything to help the war effort. Dogs pulled carts loaded with machine guns, ammunition, and other supplies. They scoured battlefields to help medics locate wounded men. Dogs delivered messages between command centers and the front lines. They kept distant outposts stocked with messenger pigeons by delivering backpacks full of live birds. Dogs guarded prisoners and served as watchdogs. They even killed the rats that took up residence in the battlefield trenches and dugouts.

Poisonous gas and armored tanks (below) were used for the first time during World War I. Humans wore gas masks for protection, and so did combat animals, from horses to mules to service dogs (left). Robert Conroy ordered Stubby a French-made dog mask, but the device had to be modified to protect the unique American-breed profile of his four-footed friend.

Soldiers traveled with their own supplies and weapons, including heavy pieces of field artillery (above, an encampment of the Fourth Division). The so-called railroad gun (left) moved separately, via train. Its shells could travel for miles even if tracks didn't reach the front.

he opposing armies traded frequent rounds of artillery fire. Conroy and the other soldiers learned that the Germans favored three sizes of shells. The so-called minnie was a slow-moving 50-pound explosive that was lobbed skyward like a giant football by a gun that emitted a loud popping noise as it fired. Terrified soldiers studied the shell's arching descent and scattered, hoping to avoid catastrophic injury. The Germans' largest guns heaved enormous 210-mm shells at the Allies. These devices created 30-foot craters and deafening shock waves when they reached ground. Worst of all, perhaps, were the so-called whiz-bangs, smaller 88-mm shells. These rounds landed without warning because they traveled faster than the speed of sound. Anyone who survived the impact of the shell had to then endure the horrifying shriek that followed in its path.

The Allied shells made distinct sounds, too, including the rapid-fire barking noise of departing 75-mm shells, the lusty roar as larger guns fired, and the reverberating boom of mammoth guns mounted on flatbed railway cars. Accounts vary on how Stubby handled all this racket. With his sensitive dog ears, he could hear the incoming rounds before the humans could. At the start of fresh barrages, he would bark an alarm of warning. Some say he howled throughout the bombardments that followed; others report he "never yelped." Some barrages seem to have left him trembling all over; others not so much. Some stories suggest the dog raced back and forth along the trenches; others indicate he held his ground, whether in the trenches with Conroy or sheltering alone in dugout bunkers. Truth be told, he probably did all of the above and more.

Conroy particularly worried about how to keep Stubby safe from gas attacks. The Germans had begun firing canisters of poisonous gas at enemy troops in April of 1915. Different types of gas caused different reactions—from vomiting to rashes to blindness to burning of the lungs. Serious exposure could be fatal, and plenty of soldiers died because of the poisonous gases. Others became disfigured or disabled. Soldiers began wearing gas masks, which helped protect them, but the devices weren't perfect.

Stubby had a gas mask, too, and he had a unique ability to sense when a gas attack was about to begin. Sounding his barked alarm, he would race through the network of underground trenches and bunkers to warn his human friends. On one occasion the dog spotted an off-duty soldier fast asleep in a dugout, and he stirred the man awake. Although some gas reached the pair before they could be protected by their masks, they avoided becoming seriously hurt. The grateful soldier, Sgt. John J. Curtin, later wrote a poem praising Stubby. One verse began, "He always knew when to duck the shells, and buried his nose at the first gas smells."

Soldiers adapted to the stresses of life on the front lines as well as they could. Camp cooks tried to keep their kitchens running through rounds of shelling. If necessary, food was prepared at a safe distance from the battlefields, and mules hauled it to the trenches in large metal containers. Supply officers tracked down local sources of food. When cooks received apples, they made apple fritters. When they received fresh vegetables—"potatoes, onions, turnips, celery, and cabbages"—they made stew. When fresh food ran low, they turned to crates of preserved food, including a seemingly endless supply of canned corned beef. One soldier in Conroy's regiment wrote home praising the French-made bread that was provided to the men, "big round loaves made from whole wheat, very nutritious and welcome to a hungry man." Stubby would have dined on soup bones, kitchen scraps, gifts from soldiers, and general foraging.

Whether or not Stubby ate the rats he killed in the trenches is unknown, but he did include rat patrol as one of his services. Rats were everywhere. They feasted on the debris of the camp and could grow as large as cats. The vermin ran through the trenches fearlessly, crawling over sleeping soldiers in their endless hunts for food. Stubby's terrier genes made him a natural hunter, and the trenches he patrolled were bound to have been home to fewer rats than those that lacked the services of a hunting dog.

Stubby couldn't help with another creature that invaded the trenches: lice. These tiny insects feed on human blood, and the parasites loved the crowded, dirty conditions of the war front. Soldiers might go for weeks without showering or changing clothes, so the lice feasted on their hosts, clinging to the men's hair, biting their skin, and triggering intense itchiness. Thick infestations of the so-called cooties could keep someone awake all night with their tireless creeping and nipping.

After spending about six weeks on the front lines, Conroy's Yankee Division earned a brief rest, and Conroy received a promotion to the rank of private, 1st class. By early April the doughboys were back at the northeastern front, this time near Toul. Once again the Americans helped the French repel German advances. On April 20, 1918, enemy forces rushed the Allied lines near the community of Seicheprey. Two companies of the 102nd Infantry became cut off from the rest of their regiment and were almost completely destroyed in an assault that lasted 18 hours. Machine Gun Parker ordered everyone from the headquarters company to reinforce the weakened lines, fearing that the Germans might break through the damaged defenses. Conroy and Stubby took their places in the trenches with the other soldiers.

As the fighting progressed, the German assault collapsed, and the enemy began to retreat. During what seemed like the end

"It seemed as though he had made up his mind to go, regardless of consequences, and his enthusiasm never wavered."

—J. Robert Conroy, reflecting on Stubby's participation in World War I

Soldiers dug underground bunkers, also known as "funk holes," wherever the terrain permitted (above, an Army truck passes a hillside network of dugouts).

of the conflict, Stubby left the shelter of his trench to cruise the battlefield. Then, unexpectedly, a shell exploded nearby. Shrapnel, or the metal fragments created by the weapon's exploding shell, struck the animal in the chest under his left leg. Stubby howled, and Conroy is said to have crawled from the trenches to rescue him.

The wound was serious, but Conroy did his best to offer immediate first aid. Soon afterward, his company was ordered back to headquarters. When Conroy appeared carrying the wounded animal, a regimental doctor treated him further, then ordered Stubby to be placed inside an ambulance beside other wounded soldiers. Whether the dog was conscious or not is unrecorded, but it is easy to imagine that a lump must have formed in Conroy's throat as he watched the vehicle drive away, vanishing into the darkness of the night.

3

Ⓧ22343

"If we can't get a dog we'll take a goat,
or a cat, or a pig, a rabbit, a sheep,
or, yes, even a wildcat. We'll take
anything for a trench companion—
but give us a DOG first."

—Lt. Ralph Kynoch of the Gordon Highlanders
of Scotland, during the First World War

IN THE TRENCHES

The ambulance drove its charges to a hospital stationed a safe distance from the fighting. Some of its medical staff members may already have known Stubby. At the very least his wounded comrades must have added their pleas for his care, so doctors and nurses tended to the four-legged combatant. An Army surgeon removed the shrapnel still embedded in Stubby's body and stitched his wounds closed. Another staff member dressed the area with antiseptic and bandages. Then Stubby was nestled into a safe place to rest.

Robert Conroy and other members of the 102nd worried a great deal about their injured friend. "For days there was deep gloom in the outfit lest Stubby should not get well," noted a subsequent account of the injury. As Conroy later noted, though, Stubby "was like the proverbial cat; he seemed to have many lives." It took six weeks, but the injured friend of the 102nd eventually made a full recovery. Near the end of his confinement, Stubby felt well enough to start touring the aisles of wounded soldiers at the hospital, charming the men with his sunny disposition and his toughness. If Stubby could recover, the patients may have thought, so could they.

Trenches offered soldiers some safety from gunfire (at left, hiding under leafy camouflage), but they provided no shelter from poisonous gas (above, a demonstration on the use of gas masks).

It was June before Stubby rejoined Conroy and the 102nd Regiment. By then the 26th Division had been on battlefronts almost constantly since early February. French and American troops continued to repulse German attacks during weeks of skirmishes at defensive points in the Champagne region of northeastern France. Conroy and Stubby delivered written messages between Allied forces and helped to gather information about the strengths and movements of the enemy. It would have been dangerous work.

At some point, either during the war or soon afterward, Conroy started a scrapbook about Stubby and their wartime experiences. The oversize, leather-bound book still exists. One page displays an assortment of snapshots grouped around the heading, "Stubby at Beaumont France," one of the places where the pair were stationed during the first half of 1918. Here is Stubby, tongue hanging out, head cocked to one side, standing on a wooden walkway. There is Conroy with Stubby, the dog perched on the legs of the squatting man, his head posed regally beside Conroy's smiling face. Elsewhere Stubby and Conroy appear with other soldiers.

In the most personal shot, the two stand beneath a tree. It is summertime, and the man and his dog could be anywhere, except for the fact that one of them is dressed in a military uniform, including knee-high field boots. Stubby stands on his hind legs with his front paws resting on Conroy's left thigh. The dog's snout just comes level with the bottom of the man's jacket. Conroy looks down at the dog and wears a joyful smile on his face. Stubby returns the gaze with equal intensity. Their bond of affection is evident.

Elsewhere Conroy has pasted a sketch in the book that was drawn in pencil by a fellow doughboy. The artist captioned his work: "Drawing of a dugout in Beaumont under our observation post." The illustration shows a soldier, probably Robert Conroy, propped up in his underground bed, reading a book. One can just make out the head of a dog, nestled in the blankets beside him.

As special as Stubby was, he was not the only mascot for the 102nd or in the military. When Stubby returned from his hospital stay, he must have met Mademoiselle Fanny. Edward Simpson, the cook for K Company, had bought the white goat in May. Simpson adored her and reputedly made Fanny clothes and put her to bed at night. Donkeys, birds, cats, and kittens served as mascots throughout the armed forces, too. A squadron of American fighter pilots even adopted a pair of lion cubs.

By midsummer the Germans were running out of energy, fresh troops, and ideas. The Allies had stopped every thrust of their drive and prevented them from breaking through the French lines. Meanwhile, more than 200,000 Americans were reaching France

DRAWING OF A DUGOUT IN BEAUMONT
UNDER OUR OBSERVATION POST

H. A. BINGHAM

Conroy (with Stubby at left and, probably, above) and the other doughboys dressed in olive-green-colored uniforms. All the men of the 26th Division wore patches on their sleeves bearing the letters YD, for Yankee Division. Rags (below), a stray French dog adopted by an American soldier, gained fame in the war, too.

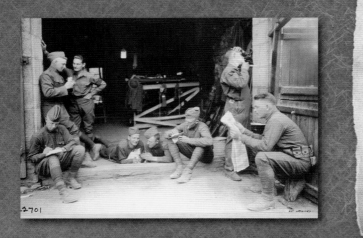

Military photographers documented ordinary moments from the war (left, a posed shot of wholesome off-duty pastimes, complete with a pet kitten). Wartime showers were few and far between (top, before bath time; below, afterward). "Their 'cooties' are gone," wrote a photographer (below), adding that the lice-free men are "going 'home' as merry as small boys from a school picnic."

every month, swelling the numbers and stamina of the Allied forces. In mid-July the tide of the war began to turn as these troops started to push back against the Germans. The Yankee Division added its weight to the counteroffensive, and the united armies began to reclaim territory long held by the opposition.

Support troops advanced right along with the rest of the 26th Division, so Conroy, Stubby, and even Mademoiselle Fanny began hiking eastward. As the soldiers moved, they began gaining not just ground but prisoners of war. Conroy's intelligence unit helped manage the identification and security of the captured German soldiers. The work suited Stubby. The dog quickly learned to recognize enemy soldiers using his sight, smell, and other senses. The glimpse of the ceremonial spiked *Pickelhaube* helmet of a German officer, for example, could provoke Stubby to bark ferociously. When the 102nd brought in prisoners, Stubby would follow alongside the arriving captives, adding his bark—and, if needed, his bite—to anyone unwise enough to stray out of line.

Those instincts served Stubby well when he performed another of his duties, too: helping to find wounded soldiers on the battlefield. Stubby didn't waste time leading medical teams to enemy wounded; he went straight for Allied fighters. The capable mascot shared a dog's instincts for recognizing if someone was dead or alive, so he could help medics and Red Cross workers reach the wounded more efficiently. In addition, his sharp sense of smell made him better than humans at finding soldiers hidden from sight, whether they lay in a field of thigh-high wheat or obscured in rough terrain.

Casualties ran high as soldiers pushed forward under intense shelling and machine-gun fire. Many lay grievously wounded on the battlefields. When Stubby found an injured man, he might stay with him, comforting him while the pair waited for human help. At other times he would keep watch with a dying soldier, offering companionship during the man's last moments of consciousness.

Finally, in early August of 1918, the 26th Division earned a break from fighting. Its forces had been in war zones almost without stop for six months. The men must have been exhausted. They'd watched whole companies collapse along the Chemin des Dames, and thousands of soldiers be killed or wounded. Surely their nerves were on edge, between the trauma of death and the mayhem of shooting and shelling. They were ready for a rest, some regular meals, and probably most of all, a bath!

Not just any bath would do, though, thanks to the soldiers' number one personal enemy: lice. The Army set up mobile disinfecting stations to meet the men's sanitation challenges. When the men met up with one of these roving stations, they started by stripping off all of their clothes, including underwear. Worn-out clothing was discarded; the rest of it was laundered in a special pressurized chamber filled with hot steam. While their clothes washed, the men cleaned their hair and showered. Weather permitting, they washed outdoors at portable rows of showerheads. Then they coated themselves in a smoky-smelling disinfecting solution before they put on fresh clothes. "Note the happy appearance of these men as they are about to leave" the laundry area, observed a service member tasked with documenting the process.

About this time Stubby earned a uniform, too. After the dog and his unit helped to liberate the French town of Château-Thierry, scores of its female residents used needle and thread to express their gratitude to the charming mascot. First they made Stubby a jacket out of soft, strong chamois leather, light brown in color. The jacket was designed to fasten under Stubby's neck with a pair of decorative buttons and snap shut under the dog's belly. Then the women sewed braided cord onto the coat, forming the words "Stubby" and "102nd U.S. INF." on what would

cover the dog's left flank. They sewed official YD service patches on the jacket's shoulder areas, too. Finally they created a colorful decorative emblem out of silk thread and sewed it onto the back of the coat. Many hands contributed stitches to the design—a wreath of interconnected flags, one for each of the nations united under the Allied war effort.

Thus outfitted, Stubby and Conroy set off on a ten-day leave to visit Paris. Their official travel documents carried both of their names, making them inseparable, officially and otherwise. On one occasion during their stay in the French capital the

Stubby's scrapbook featured sheets of large, thick black paper. When Conroy added captions, he wrote in white ink, using graceful cursive penmanship. Stubby filled the pages (far left, wearing his jacket; near left, with Conroy, standing, and an ambulance crew).

distinctive pair of sightseers attracted the attention of two sisters. They crossed paths near the city's famed Arc de Triomphe, or the Arch of Triumph, and Stubby hit it off particularly well with the younger girl. The children paused to pet and admire the well-dressed mascot, then prepared to cross the adjacent street. But Stubby nudged the younger sister with a request for more attention, and the girls lingered to pet him further. Suddenly a runaway horse and buggy appeared from around a corner and rushed past them at the intersection. Without the distraction of Stubby, the girls would have found themselves in the crazed path of the unattended horse. Thus, even when off duty, Stubby was credited with performing heroic services.

Conroy and Stubby returned to their unit in early September and before mid-month the pair were back at the front. This time the 26th Division helped clear Germans from a region near St. Mihiel, France; they captured 15,000 prisoners in four days, giving Stubby plenty of opportunities to nip at the trouser legs of enemy soldiers. Then the Yankee Division joined what Allied commanders hoped would become the final operation of the

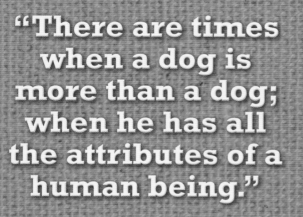

> ## "There are times when a dog is more than a dog; when he has all the attributes of a human being."
>
> —Editorial about Stubby from the
> *New Britain Herald*, published in 1926

war: the Meuse-Argonne campaign. This effort earned its name because of two battlefield landmarks, the Meuse River and the Argonne Forest. In the days leading up to the campaign, more than half a million American soldiers secretly moved into positions across the 30-mile-long battlefront. The Yankee Division contributed to the plan by preparing for a diversionary attack some distance away from the central battlefront.

The Meuse-Argonne campaign was supposed to be over in a matter of days. Instead, it lasted more than six weeks. Rains fell frequently, creating perpetual mud.

Soldiers ate cold food, endured endless shelling, and made countless deadly charges toward well-positioned machine-gun nests. Maneuvers took place at all times of day or night and under every condition, favorable or not. Sometimes banks of fog allowed the men to creep forward unseen. At other times the fog lifted unexpectedly, leaving the men as exposed as targets at a shooting gallery. The campaign was costly, unnerving, exhausting, and demoralizing.

It was during the Yankee Division's diversionary attack that Stubby performed what many regarded as his most notable wartime achievement: He captured a

GERMANS IN THE "ARGONNE"

Soldiers purchased souvenir cards that portrayed scenes of wartime destruction using colored threads (above left, Verdun Cathedral in 1916). The classic German spiked helmet, or _Pickelhaube_ (worn above), went out of fashion during the war.

German soldier. Readers can debate whether the man was a German spy, creeping forward to survey the American lines, or a disoriented soldier cut off from his retreating unit—both scenarios have been claimed. Either way, when Stubby spotted the man, he barked an alarm, then prepared to attack. Ignoring the soldier's efforts to befriend him, Stubby advanced menacingly. When the man turned to run, the athletic dog lunged after him, knocked him down, and sank his teeth into the seat of the soldier's pants. Stubby held on until human reinforcements arrived, tipped off by the dog's initial barking.

Stubby earned great praise for this feat. Some say he was made an official sergeant in the U.S. Army, a claim that inspired his eventual nickname, Sergeant Stubby. The lack of sergeant stripes on the dog's "uniform" calls this claim into question, however. Even if he didn't earn a military rank during the war, Stubby did receive high praise. On September 26, 1918, Gen. Clarence Edwards, as commander of the Yankee Division, recognized the mascot for "gallantry," most likely in response to his capture of the German soldier. A few days later, Conroy earned another promotion and became an Army corporal.

Even if Stubby didn't trot away from the feat with sergeant stripes, he did earn a souvenir. American soldiers loved to collect keepsakes after a battle, everything from buttons cut from German military uniforms to firearms to German medals. One of the most coveted finds was an Iron Cross, the German medal for excellence in military service. Stubby's captive had earned an Iron Cross, but he lost it to his captor when he became a prisoner of war. Eventually, Conroy added the medal to Stubby's jacket, displaying it so that it hung, disrespectfully, over the dog's rear end.

In mid-October commanders halted the relentless assaults of the Meuse-Argonne campaign and regrouped for one final push. The Yankee Division took up positions on the main battlefront and was on hand when the Allies renewed their coordinated attacks on November 1. The next day, when Conroy was "wounded in action slightly" by poison gas, so was Stubby. It was Conroy's first wartime injury, and he recuperated together with Stubby at a nearby Army hospital. When the pair returned to duty, only the timing of Germany's defeat remained in question.

Medical staff members improvised and adapted as the fighting shifted in intensity and from place to place (opposite page, soldiers on stretchers fill a bombed-out church). The military established more permanent facilities, too. When Conroy caught the Spanish flu after the war, he spent eight days recovering at a hospital in Paris.

On Sunday, November 10, 1918, soldiers learned that an armistice, or cease-fire, would begin the next morning. Thus, on the date of 11-11 soldiers anticipated the end of fighting at the hour of 11 o'clock. Some soldiers hunkered down to keep safe as the time approached. Others charged forward after ambitious officers ordered them to continue taking ground, whatever the costs. Some batteries shut down their guns. Others raced to see if they could fire off every shell that remained in their arsenals. In places artillery guns became so hot that layers of protective paint began to cook off of the discharge barrels. When the guns finally ceased firing at the appointed hour, one soldier observed in his diary, "The silence is oppressive. It weighs in on one's eardrums."

Soldiers emerged from their trenches and began to celebrate. In Conroy's unit, "hundreds of friends crowded around Stubby," according to a subsequent news account. "Many credited him with causing the gods to yield the good luck of victory." The battle lines stretched for miles, and at more than one location, the former enemies came out to interact in the

"No Man's Land" that had divided them, akin to the way opposing teams meet on the field after a fierce football game. In some cases they swapped souvenirs. At one location the former foes worked together to find their wounded. Then the men collected firewood, built a bonfire, and gathered around it for warmth.

Even with defeat, plenty of German soldiers felt like celebrating: They, too, had survived the war. After darkness fell, some of them improvised rounds of festive fireworks by shooting signal flares into the night sky. That evening the colors lost their wartime meanings of warning, attack, and distress. This time the intermingled rainbow of sparks signaled one thing and one thing only: The fighting is finished!

"He is a fighting bulldog of the old Y.D.
And is the joy and pride of our company.
When we take him back to the U.S.A.,
Stubby will hold the stage,
night and day."

—Verse from a poem composed by Sgt. John J. Curtin, whom Stubby had saved during a gas attack, 1918

VICTORY LAP

For all the fireworks, American soldiers quickly learned they would not be rushing home. It had taken months to ferry millions of men to the front, and it would take months to send them back. Plus, the armistice represented only a cease-fire. Allies needed to keep troops near the front to make sure that the Germans weren't tempted to resume fighting. So Robert Conroy and the other soldiers climbed out of the trenches and settled into postwar camps.

Stubby was one of the lucky war dogs. The French destroyed their corps of canine service dogs, fearful that the animals would not adapt to a peaceful lifestyle. Dogs that had served other countries fared better, but few gained the attention directed at Stubby. The entire Yankee Division now claimed him as its mascot. He was well loved, widely known, and gaining fame with ease.

When Woodrow Wilson visited the Yankee Division in France on Christmas Day, 1918, the President met Stubby and shook his paw. When soldiers received wound stripes and service bars for their uniforms, so did Stubby. When the French created medals to thank soldiers for liberating their cities, Conroy made sure that Stubby shared in the glory. Stubby's jacket became arrayed with medals from Verdun (red ribbon), St. Mihiel (gold and red ribbon),

Troops celebrated the end of the war with cheers (left page) and parades (above, Gen. John J. Pershing, commander of the American Expeditionary Force, at the Arc de Triomphe in Paris).

and Château-Thierry (white ribbon), as well as a commemorative award from the French government that hung from a peppermint-striped ribbon.

Each Allied nation issued its own victory medal, too. U.S. soldiers clipped metal bars over their medal's rainbow-patterned ribbon to identify where they had fought. Stubby's victory medal included five crossbars: Champagne-Marne, Aisne-Marne, St. Mihiel, Meuse-Argonne, and the "Defensive Sector." Stubby is credited with participating in 17 battles during those engagements. Throw in the Iron Cross that Stubby had won off his German captive, and the veteran would have looked the

part of a military hero. In fact, that's exactly how people saw Stubby: as their hero. Before long he was viewed not just as the mascot of the Yankee Division but of the entire American Expeditionary Force, representing all the troops that the U.S. had contributed to the Great War.

In March of 1919 Stubby and Conroy set off on their final furlough in France. They didn't get very far. No sooner had they reached Paris than Conroy became ill with the so-called Spanish flu, a deadly virus that killed millions after the war. Conroy ended up at a Red Cross hospital where, as he later

Stubby's uniform hung heavy with honors (far left, his jacket, and, detail, a soldier's victory medal). It included a wound stripe on the right shoulder area and a three-bar service patch on the left (near left). Each service bar signified 6 months of combat duty, or 18 total.

wrote, "a regulation barred admission of dogs." That restriction didn't stop man or beast for long, according to Conroy. "On learning Stubby's history, the doctors went into a huddle and decided that Stubby could bunk alongside the soldier's cot in a tent on the hospital grounds. Stubby had no difficulty winning the friendship of everyone at the hospital. In fact, they wanted Stubby and the soldier to stay indefinitely."

Conroy concluded his story using his usual sense of humor and the twist of Stubby's point of view. "When Stubby let them know he had already used eight days of a 14-day furlough and that he just had to see Monte Carlo, they agreed

to release him provided he took good care of the convalescing soldier." Thus liberated, Conroy and Stubby headed south to enjoy a quick look at the Mediterranean coast of France before returning on schedule to their unit. Four days later the 102nd Regiment departed France, bound for home. This time Conroy was spared the challenge of smuggling Stubby onto the ship; instead, he received permission to place the famed mascot safely aboard the *Agamemnon*.

Stubby wasn't the only animal that soldiers brought home from the front. Somehow, K Company cook Edward Simpson managed to bring Mademoiselle

Fanny on board Stubby's ship. Elsewhere in France, a corporal named Lee Duncan secured permission to bring back two German shepherd puppies he had found. (The one named Rin Tin Tin would eventually become famous by starring in silent movies.)

Other soldiers had less luck bringing home animals. Historian Edward G. Lengel recounts the horrifying fate that befell a German dachshund rescued from the trenches by a doughboy from the First Division. The soldier smuggled the dog aboard his returning ship but was later caught taking his pet for an evening walk. The man was arrested, and his dog was thrown overboard and left to drown.

When Conroy's ship reached Boston Harbor, family members, friends, and the governors of three states were there to meet it, waving flags and holding hand-lettered signs. Long-awaited hugs had to wait, though. First the men had to be demobilized, or released from duty. And they needed one final round of delousing; it took some 50 hours to clean up Conroy's regiment. Then the soldiers did what they'd become quite good at doing: They waited.

However impatient, dirty, or battle-scarred the men might have been, these soldiers were seen as the lucky ones. Plenty of their friends had died in combat or from wounds or from disease. The roster of Connecticut service members is sprinkled with starred entries that bear a blunt alphabetic code: KIA, killed in action; DW, died of wounds; DD, died of disease.

Sometimes the whiff of a story accompanies a notation: "suicide"; "vessel was torpedoed and sunk"; "accidental drowning." Some soldiers died maddeningly close to the war's end. Most entries conclude with a fact or two, perhaps the location of a grave or the identity of who first heard the news. Often the name of a mother is given, but sometimes it's a father, another relative, or simply a friend.

A short while before their discharge, some 20,000 members of the Yankee Division marched through the streets of Boston in a victory parade. Over a million people cheered the veterans for hours in freezing temperatures. Governors from five neighboring states joined Massachusetts governor Calvin Coolidge in the parade reviewing stand. General Edwards led the procession on horseback. The division's companies followed, mostly on foot, interspersed with their marching bands. Wounded soldiers rode in automobiles. Mademoiselle Fanny, guided by a rope, accompanied K Company.

Stubby walked in a place of honor with the 102nd Regiment, accompanying its color guard display of ceremonial flags. As each contingent of troops reached the reviewing stand, marchers would have responded to the parade command of "eyes right" by turning their heads toward the dignitaries in a sign of respect. Stubby understood this command, so he must have turned his head, too. Then at the

209 — MONTE-CARLO - Les Jardins.

000056

LE MANS B
ᴇ COMMOY
Ce billet doit être
rendu à l'arrivée
PRI
0.45
3ᵉ ᴅ'ORLEANS
LE MANS. B.
ᴇ COMMOY

000056

During his last trip with Stubby in France, Conroy collected postcards (above, the gardens of Monte Carlo) and other souvenirs (top right and below right, transit tickets). Days later the pair headed home on the same ship as Mademoiselle Fanny (below left).

PARIS-MONTPᵉˢˢᴇ 7ᴱ Bᴬᵁ (G.I)
LE MANS
ETAT
LA
PRIX:
3ᶠ 65
00126

Cⁱᵉ des Tramways de Nice et du Littoral
BILLET DE
30 cent.
D
05712

Stubby
$62.50

Stubby's first
envelope for three
days appearance
at the Bijou Theater
New Haven Conn
May 1-2-3-1919.

People loved Stubby whether
on parade (top), when making
news (above, earning "three
bones a day" from the YMCA),
or on stage. Stubby received
$62.50 a day during his
vaudeville debut—a whopping
sum at the time (right, his
first pay envelope).

appropriate time he would have faced frontward again and continued walking in formation until commanded to stop.

When Conroy received his honorable discharge from the military he was given $60 in severance pay and a red discharge badge, called a chevron, just like other doughboys. Soldiers sewed the upside-down V onto the left sleeve of their uniforms, signifying their release from military service. Stubby's uniform soon sported a discharge chevron, too. Instead of severance pay he probably received just a parting salute. When the Connecticut veterans reached their state capital of Hartford, they paraded again. An estimated 200,000 residents turned out to cheer their own, including the uniformed dog at the head of the 102nd Regiment.

The next day, Conroy and Stubby made their stage debut. Organizers for a Victory Loan fund-raiser had recruited the pair to appear at the Bijou Theatre in New Haven, Connecticut. They participated there in a vaudeville show, a popular form of live entertainment before the era of movie palaces and television. Notices bragged that patrons would see "the most famous dog in the American army," other live acts, and the new silent film *Captain Kidd, Jr.,* starring movie idol Mary Pickford. As part of the show a duo named Walker and Texas danced and performed rope tricks. A popular comedy team called Ryan and Healey told jokes and sang. Another pair acted out a skit,

and a woman entertained the audience with humorous songs.

Perhaps the applause that accompanied Conroy and Stubby when they walked onto the stage seemed no more rattling to the dog than the chaos of trench warfare. Conroy must have told the audience some of Stubby's adventures and asked his fellow veteran to salute and perform other military maneuvers. The pair repeated their appearances three times daily for three days. Other vaudeville engagements followed.

Stubby led one last homecoming parade—in Conroy's hometown of New Britain—and then the pair settled down there. Conroy moved into the home of his eldest sister, her husband, and their two children. Most of his siblings lived there, too. When Conroy tried his hand as a traveling salesman, Stubby stayed behind and played with Conroy's niece and nephew. "Nobody could mind Stubby," Conroy's sister told a curious news reporter. "He's a good beast, and the baby loves him a great deal. They are regular chums."

In early 1920 Conroy nominated the dog for a new award being offered by the judges of the annual Eastern Dog Club show in Boston: Hero Dog. "He's probably a mutt," a judge said after Stubby won the award. Then, referring to all the well-groomed, purebred competitors in the rest of the show, he added: "But he's done more than all the rest put together."

"Whether the Creator planned it so or environment and human companionship have made it so, men may learn richly through the love and fidelity of a brave and devoted dog."

—Warren G. Harding, during his years as a U.S. senator, offering praise to dogs after learning a favorite dog had died

AT EASE, SGT. STUBBY

Any other war story would have ended there, with a gracious retirement from the public's eye. But not Stubby's. The mascot's fame grew, in part because Robert Conroy nurtured the dog's reputation at strategic moments, just like a proud papa. But Stubby's story had a life of its own, too. One spot of glory led to the next. One headline fed another. Unbelievable moments added up until Stubby seemed known to just about everyone.

It helped that the pair moved to the bustling news hub of Washington, D.C., around the fall of 1920. Conroy and Stubby took up residence at 1600 Rhode Island Avenue with a group of Army buddies. They nicknamed themselves the Carry On Club, making playful use of the military command "carry on," which officers gave soldiers at the end of official interactions. Stubby carried on by trading in his war uniform for an athletic uniform when Conroy enrolled at the law school of Georgetown University. Stubby's jacket bore one decoration, the letter *G*, and he wore the blue-and-gray outfit whenever he shared the field with the football team.

Stubby supported the Georgetown University Hilltoppers after the war by serving as mascot for the football team (left page). His fame inevitably drew crowds (above, on the capitol grounds, Hartford, Connecticut).

The Hilltoppers, as they were then known, had had mascots before, but none of the others had been quite like Stubby. Stubby made a quick study of his new surroundings and added fresh skills to his arsenal. He loved to chase after the leather football and would butt it with his head when he caught up to it. Then he would pursue the moving ball all over again. Fans loved his antics, and soon his performance became a regular attraction during the halftime break in home games.

In the spring of 1921 the Humane Education Society, an organization now known as the American Humane Association, added to Stubby's fame. For starters, organizers plunked the dog down on a featured float in its "Be Kind to Animals Week" parade in the nation's capital. Horses, dozens of other dogs, even sheep and parrots, took part in the event. Laddie Boy, an Airedale owned by President Warren G. Harding and his First Lady, led the procession aboard a horse-drawn parade float. Stubby followed, seated beside a young girl. Attired in his medal-laden jacket, sporting a harness that displayed an American flag, his image appeared in newspapers as far away as New York City.

Then the society created an award to recognize the dog's "bravery under fire" during rescue work in France. Movie cameras whirled, and camera flashbulbs popped as no less a dignitary than Gen. John J. Pershing, commander of the American Expeditionary Force in Europe, pinned the gold medal onto the dog's uniform. Conroy found humor in the way that Stubby's fame opened doors, even

at the general's Washington headquarters. He later recalled how, before the ceremony, "At the entrance to that building [Stubby] was told by guards that dogs are not allowed to enter. Stubby quietly told them he was expected at the offices of the General of the Armies, John J. Pershing. After a telephone inquiry, the bar was removed."

That same summer Stubby met U.S. President Warren G. Harding while attending a White House garden party for wounded veterans. "Mrs. Harding held Stubby's leash for ten minutes," Conroy reported. Now Stubby had met two Presidents. He would go on to meet a third, Calvin Coolidge, during a later visit to the White House.

As Stubby's fame grew, so did the tall tales about him. Sometimes journalists slaughtered the facts of his life. In one story the New York Times explained that Stubby had gotten his name because, "in the World War part of a leg was shot off." Some reporters called the dog by the wrong name; errors included "Stubbie," "Stuffy," and "Hubby." Others referred to Stubby as "she." Reporters exaggerated how often Stubby had been wounded. One even claimed that "Stuffy" was such a "toughy" that "he happened to stop five bullets."

Rumors swirled. Stubby had started the Christmas Truce, where opposing sides had stepped out of the trenches to socialize. (False. The Christmas Truce occurred in 1914, long before Stubby

Stubby's fame grew (right, one of his many news stories) after Gen. John J. Pershing awarded the dog a medal for bravery (above). Reporters teased of a rivalry between Stubby and other dogs (below left, Marine mascot Sergeant Major Jiggs; below right, Laddie Boy with President Warren G. Harding).

'Twas "Stubby's" Day

SPECIAL DISPATCH TO THE ENQUIRER.

Washington, July 6.—This was a great day in the career of "Stubby," canine hero of the World War. With motion pictures focused upon him, he was decorated for "bravery under fire" by no less a personage than General John J. Pershing.

The medal was provided by the district branch of the Humane Educational Society as a souvenir of its recent "kindness to animals" parade.

Stubby proved to be a modest hero. He received the decoration with a slight aggitation of the abbreviated appendage from which he derives his name, but in no other way did he betray his pride at the honors showered upon him. And to prove that being decorated by the leader of America's victorious forces had left him the same old unpretentious Stubby, he barked a Democratic greeting to Laddie Boy as he passed the White House on his return from the ceremony.

Of course Laddie Boy also has a medal from the Socity, but it was presented besause he happened to be the Presidential dog and not for any conspicuous gallantry on the field of battle.

Stubby has the distinction of being the only dog that went overseas with the troops and returned. He was in 17 engagements with the Twenty-sixth Division, and once was wounded. His master is J. Robert Conroy, of New Haven, Conn., a former member of the Twenty-sixth, who was present at the ceremony to-day.

Following Stubby's decoration the Society presented to General Pershing a gold mounted billfold in the compliments to his horse kedron.

It's a (famous) dog's life, from amusement rides (top, with Robert Conroy and, probably, Conroy's twin sisters) to visits with Presidents (below, souvenir tag from representing the Carry On Club at a 1921 Harding garden party). In 1924 Stubby visited the White House to see Calvin Coolidge (left, two Boston terriers help entertain the retired President).

IDENTIFICATION TAG

WHITE HOUSE PARTY

June 8th, 1921.

CarryOn

reached Europe.) Stubby had saved the town of Château-Thierry. (Could be. After all, why did so many of the town's women make him that jacket?) Stubby's antics on the Georgetown University athletic field inspired the whole idea for a halftime show at football games. (Why not? If it isn't true, it should be!)

Stubby didn't charm everyone. One veteran complained that the dog was getting better treatment than returning soldiers, earning "three bones a day" through the YMCA when some "ex soldiers are starving in the streets of our big cities." Another man took exception with all the credit being given to a dog when so many men had fought, suffered, and died without comparable acclaim. He concluded: "If this Boston bull did so much and the boys didn't do anything, why not send an army of bull pups the next time" there is a war? Conroy dutifully pasted the men's published letters of complaint into Stubby's scrapbook. Then he added his positive spin to their protests with this handwritten caption: "Criticism of Stubby which proves he is famous."

Few veterans resented Stubby's fame and care, though. Anyone who met the mascot appreciated him, and, over time, thousands and thousands of veterans came to know and love Stubby. Conroy and his famous charge became the guests of honor at countless military reunions, whether in Washington, D.C., back in

Connecticut, or on the road. Year after year Stubby and Conroy took train trips to attend national meetings of the American Legion, the service organization for World War I veterans. Minneapolis. Kansas City. New Orleans. Omaha. Stubby saw them all. And he paraded in all of them, too, always leading a color guard, with a tiny flag waving above his back, offering "eyes right" at the reviewing stand, just like the other doughboys. Newspaper accounts filled Stubby's scrapbook, and souvenir pins began to dangle below the trim line of his jacket, like fringe.

In between all the moments of fame, travel, and work, Conroy and Stubby made sure to have plain old fun, too. Even a visit to the Washington Monument became an adventure with Stubby along, as Conroy noted when he wrote about one of their outings in a brief memoir. "One day when Stubby was near the Washington Monument, a friend carried him under his raincoat past the guards and part way up the stairs. Stubby then walked to the top of the monument, and, after looking over the city of Washington, he walked down the stairs and passed the guards, who could not understand how that dog got by them. Of course, they did not know it was a minor operation for Stubby."

Stubby retired from his mascot duties at Georgetown University around 1923, in part because Conroy's study at the law school was drawing to a close. Conroy had already transitioned to a job on Capitol Hill in the office of a Connecticut congressman. Plus, the truth was, Stubby was beginning to show his age. Yes, he could still fit into his uniform—a claim that would make many aging veterans jealous—but he was slowing down. After all, Stubby had shadowed Conroy for seven years by then, and he'd weathered who knew what in the uncalculated time that preceded their friendship.

Even as he aged, Stubby remained in the public's eye. He attended more dog shows, helped with an Easter egg roll, allowed his portrait to be painted, participated in more charity events, and took part in further parades. The old Army mascot never tired of being around other soldiers. A reporter from the *New Britain Herald* described a visit the aging Stubby made to the Eddy-Glover Post of the American Legion, in Conroy's hometown. When Stubby first entered the packed room, the reporter notes that Stubby "looked around, apparently bewildered." Then the dog spotted a color guard. "Seeing the one thing that he recognized, he trotted soberly over to where the uniformed men were standing and reared back on his haunches in a perfect canine salute."

In the early months of 1926, the tireless Conroy sought one more honor for his aging companion. This one was personal: Conroy wanted Stubby to become an official member of that Eddy-Glover Post in New Britain. The mascot had been made

an honorary member years before. Now Conroy submitted an application, complete with membership dues ($4) and "Stubby's seal" (an inked impression of Stubby's paw print). That honor became the last one bestowed on Stubby, for suddenly, all at once, the celebrated mascot was no more.

Around midnight on March 16, 1926, some eight years after entering the front lines of France, Stubby died. With an estimated age of 11 or 12 years, he succumbed for no better reason than being old. Stubby drew his final breaths

> **"Stubby only a dog? Nonsense! Stubby was the visible incarnation of the great spirit that hovered over the 26th."**
>
> —Editorial, published in the *New Britain Herald* following Stubby's death, 1926

When he wasn't traveling, Stubby lived with Conroy in Washington, D.C. (above, with a portrait artist).

while cradled in the arms of his best friend, Robert Conroy. When Conroy's regimental commander, Machine Gun Parker, heard the news, he expressed his sadness. Parker—the man who once joked that only Stubby could get away with talking back to him during the war—spoke for his troops when he said of Stubby's loss, simply: "He will be mourned as sincerely as any other of our comrades."

Conroy recorded only a few words about the death of the friend who had been his closest companion during and after the war. "All who knew him will grieve over his 'going west,' but especially the writer," he wrote to their fellow veterans. Conroy observed that Stubby's experiences "paralleled the common lot of every soldier who served actively abroad." Then he added: "His passing on was a peaceful end to an adventurous life, and it seemed as though his last message was one of gratitude to all who had loved, and been kind to him."

"The boys loved him and now that the tiny life is ended, a real link with the Great Adventure is snapped."

—Editorial, *New Haven Journal Courier*, following the death of Stubby in 1926

"My grandfather always said Stubby adopted him,"
remembers Curtis Deane, the grandson of J. Robert Conroy.
Almost a century after the bond formed between Stubby and
Conroy, the man's 65-year-old grandson helps document his
family's history. Deane notes that Conroy "was always very quiet about the details of what
he did during the war. He'd just say he was with Stubby," recalls Deane. "That man was
devoted to that dog. Stubby may have been what got him through the war." Deane is
too young, of course, to have met Stubby, but his grandfather kept Stubby's memory alive
long after his friend's death. "Stubby was his avocation," explains Deane.

When Stubby died, the *New York Times* ran a lengthy obituary about the mascot.
So did the *Washington Post*. Stubby's death made headlines far and wide, in fact.
But Conroy believed that Stubby deserved more lasting recognition: He wanted the
famed mascot to become part of a museum. Conroy set his sights on the Smithsonian
Institution; immediately after Stubby's death, he arranged for one of its taxidermists
to preserve Stubby. As part of this process, a plaster cast was made of Stubby's body.
His perishable remains were then cremated, placed in a metal container, and
embedded within that cast. Stubby's furry hide covered its exterior.

**Stubby (above, during the
1921 Humane Education
Society parade) now stands
(left) alongside famed carrier
pigeon Cher Ami and other
World War I artifacts in the
Smithsonian's National
Museum of American History.**

This stuffed Stubby made the rounds of American
Legion conventions, stood on display in shop
windows, and earned long-term exhibit space at
the Red Cross Museum in Washington, D.C. Decades
passed before Conroy retrieved Stubby from the
Red Cross and took charge of him once more.

For years Curtis Deane visited his grandfather every Easter in Florida (left, with Robert Conroy standing far left). Before his death, Conroy entrusted Deane with the few mementos of Stubby's life that he had not given to the Smithsonian, including some cherished photographs.

Then he and Stubby had one last adventure together.

On an early morning in 1954, when Conroy, then an attorney, was in his early 60s, a fire broke out in his high-rise residential complex. Ordered to leave the building, Conroy departed wearing a coat over his pajamas. In his arms he carried Stubby.

Two years later the Smithsonian agreed to add Stubby to its collections. Conroy gave the museum all the dog's accessories, too: his brass-studded collar, the leather harness that had displayed a tiny flag when Stubby marched in parades, his jacket and its many decorations. And Conroy gave the museum the scrapbook that he had painstakingly kept about his dog. The oversized volume held some 90 pages of memories. One could turn back the heavy leather cover, embossed in gold with the letters "Stubby A.E.F. Mascot," and step into a world of train travel, black-and-white news, and, well, love.

Parting with such treasures must have been bittersweet for Conroy. On the one hand, he knew his dog's memory stood a better chance of being kept alive in the hands of Smithsonian curators. On the other hand, the aging veteran was letting go of his most visible links to the being who had kept him company through the darkest days of the war.

Today, we understand the ways that service animals improve the mental health of soldiers in war zones. There is a comfort that comes from having an unfailingly loyal companion during such stressful times. It took decades, but eventually dogs became an increasingly important part of the American military family. Now, military service dogs stand guard as sentries, lead patrols, and detect bombs. They serve as mascots, and they behave like friends. They work tirelessly and endure unimaginable chaos. They even care for service members who have returned home, soothing veterans as they recover from the trauma that can be triggered by the horrors of war.

We've learned to press dogs into service in other ways, too. They guide the sightless. They serve as rescue workers following natural disasters. They patrol with police officers. They use their noses to find everything from illegal drugs to lost persons to dangerous explosives. They even help scientists track endangered species and work with conservationists to protect animals from illegal hunting. They work hard—like a dog, as we say—and they serve without complaint.

During the decades that followed Stubby's death, Robert Conroy married, started a family, divorced, and celebrated the arrival of grandchildren. His career

Robert Conroy worked on Capitol Hill during the 1920s (above, on the steps of the Capitol with Stubby and the dog's harness). Conroy lived to be 95 but never owned another dog.

path beyond Capitol Hill included work as an attorney, as an FBI agent, and with military intelligence.

In the decades following Conroy's gift of Stubby to the Smithsonian, the mounted dog spent many years kenneled in a packing crate on a shelf in the museum's vast storage chambers. Early on, though, Stubby was exhibited at the Arts and Industries Building, and on one occasion Conroy took his eldest grandson there to see his old friend. "He was very proud of Stubby," recalls Deane. In 2004 Stubby

Stubby wore his medal-laden jacket for special occasions and photo opportunities (above, supporting a veterans' fund-raising event).

came out of storage for good and became part of a Smithsonian military history exhibit, "The Price of Freedom."

In his later years Conroy remarried and enjoyed an active retirement in Palm Beach, Florida. He opted to bike places rather than drive; became an informal civic leader for the community; and spoke out against local discrimination, toward both African Americans and Jews. He was "a

gentleman 20 ways to Sunday," recalls Deane, noting that his grandfather never lost his temper.

As Conroy aged, the Great War became an almost forgotten conflict. Conroy lived on, enjoying excellent health well into his 90s. Then, in 1987, almost 70 years after his 1919 hospitalization for the flu, the aging veteran fell and found himself back in a hospital bed. "He was a proud man with a lot of dignity," explains Deane, and the hospital environment didn't suit him. Conroy waited for his grandson to fly in for a visit. Then, as Deane headed home, Conroy reportedly turned to his wife, and said: "Margaret, I love you very much, but I've had enough." Next, the family story goes, "he closed his eyes and died."

Although the pages of Stubby's scrapbook no longer appear in order, one can imagine that its last page could originally have been the one that displays a single black-and-white photograph. The image captures the painted portrayal of Stubby, standing in profile. Stubby, who has turned his head toward the viewer, looks serious but not emotionless. His expression seems to carry a weight with it, the duty of serving as a perennial mascot, perhaps. The eyes have a tiredness to them, even a sorrow. Maybe he, too, carries scars from the war. Maybe he senses that his life is drawing to a close. Maybe he's just tired of standing for the portrait! Regardless, his rich dark eyes seem to reflect a deep reserve of kindness. Were these emotions captured by the painter or imposed by the artist on the subject? Sorrow. Wisdom. Love. Can all those things be found in a dog?

A chorus of voices would no doubt join Robert Conroy's in saying, "Yes!"

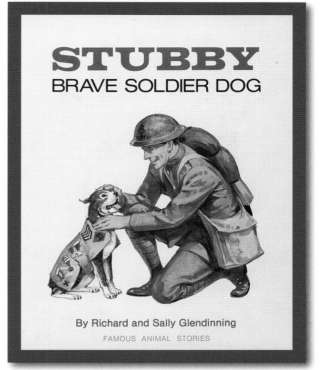

Stubby's story endured long after his death, including an account for young readers (above) published in 1978.

Time Line

1892

■ James Joseph Conroy, later known as J. Robert Conroy, is born on February 27 in New Britain, Connecticut, the third of six children.

1899

■ James P. Conroy, father of J. Robert Conroy, dies on September 25 in New Britain, Connecticut.

1913

■ Alice McAvay Conroy, mother of J. Robert Conroy, dies on March 15 in New Britain, Connecticut.

1914

■ The assassination of Archduke Francis Ferdinand on June 28 sets off events that lead to World War I.

■ The German invasion of Belgium on August 4 marks the beginning of combat for what becomes known as the Great War and World War I.

1917

■ On April 6 the United States declares war on Germany and prepares to enter the fight.

■ Conroy enlists in the Connecticut National Guard on May 21, the first step toward joining the U.S. Army. Soon after, he begins his military training on the athletic fields of Yale University in New Haven, Connecticut.

■ On June 14 Gen. John J. Pershing and his team of advisers settle in France so they can plan for the arrival of American forces later in the year.

■ A stray dog befriends Conroy and other service members during the

Conroy (left), Stubby, and a fellow soldier in 1918

summer at their training ground in Connecticut and begins to live with them.

■ Conroy's National Guard unit becomes a part of the 26th or Yankee Division of the U.S. Army; Conroy departs Connecticut with members of the 102nd Infantry in late summer, bound for Newport News, Virginia. Stubby tags along.

■ That fall, when Conroy's unit heads to Europe aboard the *Minnesota*, Conroy arranges for Stubby to be smuggled along. They reach France 26 days later and head inland for further training.

1918

■ Conroy and Stubby reach the front lines of France on February 5 to help defend battle lines along the Chemin des Dames highway. Fighting continues. Stubby experiences his first gas attack there in late March.

■ On April 5 Conroy receives his first military promotion, to private 1st class.

■ Stubby is seriously wounded by shrapnel during a battle near Seicheprey on April 20. He spends six weeks in a military hospital recovering from his injuries before rejoining Conroy and his unit.

■ That spring and summer Conroy and Stubby are based near Toul to take part in the Château-Thierry campaign, a defensive operation that turns into an offensive drive during July and early August.

■ Conroy and Stubby take part in the St. Mihiel campaign starting on September 12. The 26th Division retakes the desired territory in four days by routing Germans from the area.

■ Allied forces begin the Meuse-Argonne campaign on September 26, an undertaking designed to defeat the German forces and end the war. It lasts for weeks with varying degrees of intensity along multiple points at the front lines. The Yankee Division, including Conroy and Stubby, plays an integral part in the campaign.

■ Stubby earns commendation on September 26,

apparently for helping to capture a German soldier.

■ Conroy receives his second and final military promotion, to corporal, on September 30.

■ On November 2 Conroy is "wounded in action slightly" by poison gas when the Germans attack the Bois d'Ormont north of Verdun during the Meuse-Argonne campaign. Stubby is injured by gas at the same time. Both Conroy and Stubby make a full recovery following their brief hospitalization and return together to the battlefront.

■ Germany signs an armistice agreement with its enemies on November 11, and all combat ceases at 11 o'clock in the morning.

■ Later that fall, the Yankee Division settles into its winter quarters at Basigny, France, awaiting its return to the United States.

■ President Woodrow Wilson visits with U.S. service members at Basigny on Christmas Day, December 25. Stubby is introduced to Wilson during the visit and shakes hands with the President.

German machine gunners during World War I

1919

- On March 13 Conroy and Stubby begin a two-week furlough, intending to visit the south of France, but Conroy catches the Spanish flu and requires hospitalization in Paris. Stubby receives permission to stay with him. Conroy is discharged in time for the pair to visit Monte Carlo before their furlough ends on March 27.

- Conroy and Stubby depart France from Brest, France, on March 31, sailing on the *Agamemnon* with other members of the 102nd Regiment and the Yankee Division. They reach Boston Harbor on April 7.

- Stubby leads the 102nd Regiment in the Boston victory parade on April 25, celebrating the return of the Yankee Division.

- On April 26 Conroy receives an honorable discharge from the U.S. military. He and Stubby depart for visits and celebrations in various Connecticut cities.

- Stubby begins a three-day engagement on May 1 at the Bijou Theatre in New Haven, Connecticut, appearing with Conroy as part of a vaudeville show of live performances and other entertainment.

- On May 8 Stubby receives a lifetime membership in the YMCA, good for "three bones a day" and "a place to sleep."

- Representatives sign the Treaty of Versailles on June 28, marking the official end of World War I.

- Stubby accompanies Conroy to the first convention of the newly formed American

Stubby earns star billing for a vaudeville show.

Legion, serving veterans of World War I, when the group meets in Minneapolis, Minnesota, November 10–12.

1920

- Stubby receives the Hero Dog Award in February at the Eastern Dog Club show in Boston.

- That fall Conroy moves with Stubby to Washington, D.C. Soon after, he enrolls in the law school at Georgetown University. Stubby becomes the mascot for the university's football team and serves with the athletes for several seasons.

1921

- Stubby is awarded a "special prize" from the Boston Terrier Club in Washington, D.C., on March 7.

- Stubby and Conroy attend a party for wounded veterans, held on the grounds of the White House on June 8. They meet President Warren G. Harding and Mrs. Harding during the event.

- On July 6 Gen. John J. Pershing presents Stubby with a medal from the Humane Education Society, an animal rights group, to celebrate Stubby's work as a rescue dog during World War I and commemorate his

participation in the society's mid-May parade in the nation's capital.

- Conroy and Stubby join other veterans during October for an American Legion convention in Kansas City, Missouri. Military leaders from the Allied forces gather with veterans to dedicate the site where the Liberty Memorial will be built, commemorating the Great War. In subsequent falls Conroy and Stubby take part in American Legion conventions in New Orleans, Minneapolis, and Omaha.

1924

- On October 29 Conroy and Stubby are invited to visit the White House to meet there with President Calvin Coolidge.

1925

- Charles Ayer Whipple, the artist for the U.S. Capitol, paints a portrait of Stubby wearing his jacket and military honors.

- Conroy and Stubby attend their final American Legion convention together when they travel to Omaha, Nebraska, during October.

1926

- Stubby dies at home, cradled in Conroy's arms, on March 16. Conroy immediately makes arrangements to have the dog's remains preserved.

1927

- In December Stubby's remains go on exhibit at the headquarters of the American Red Cross, on long-term loan from Conroy.

1954

- Conroy and Stubby make the news when Conroy flees a burning high-rise in Washington, D.C., on April 21, bearing the stuffed remains of Stubby in his arms.

1956

- On May 22 Conroy presents the Smithsonian Institution with the stuffed remains of Stubby, the scrapbook he had created about the dog, Stubby's jacket and medals, and the dog's collar and harness.

Stubby's portrait hangs in Connecticut's West Haven Veterans Museum.

1987

- James Robert Conroy dies in West Palm Beach, Florida, on April 25 at the age of 95. His remains are cremated and laid to rest in that city.

2004

- Stubby goes on permanent display at the Smithsonian in the "Price of Freedom" exhibit at the National Museum of American History.

Research Notes

When I first stumbled across Stubby, I didn't believe his story was true. I was working online, and my immediate reaction was: This is a joke—these are fake posts. Then I clicked on a link hosted by the Smithsonian Institution. There he was, not just in reputable words but in the flesh, or at least the fur. The site showed Stubby's stuffed remains on display at the National Museum of American History.

My mind wouldn't let Stubby go, even as writing deadlines for a different project forced me to step off his trail. Maybe the dog was worth a book, I thought, so I printed out a reference copy of the Smithsonian material and started an idea folder labeled "Sgt. Stubby." That was 2009. I finished my original book and wrote another one, but Stubby stayed with me. Every now and then I'd return to his idea file, add a few notes, and let the topic simmer.

Finally, in 2011 I jumped in. I knew that Robert Conroy, Stubby's owner, had kept a scrapbook about his four-footed friend, and that he'd given it to the Smithsonian along with his stuffed dog. When I headed to Washington, D.C., for other research, I extended my trip to see the scrapbook. I spent an afternoon with it and took many pages of handwritten notes. Later I worked up a proposal for a book about Stubby, and when I shared it with my publisher, people at National Geographic got excited about the idea, too.

So far, so good, but rarely have I undertaken a project with such slim prospects for research. What did we have to go on? Not much! A stuffed dog, a dog-eared scrapbook, and a swirling drama of facts and fancy. But, thanks to the magic of history and hard work and plain old coincidence, a three-dimensional portrait of the past has emerged from these slim pickings.

My best break came almost a year later, when I received a packet of news clippings from a librarian at the New Britain Public Library in New Britain, Connecticut. I'd contacted the library as a matter of logical routine. Robert Conroy was from New Britain; maybe the town remembered him. Patricia Watson did know about Conroy, or at least she recognized his pal Stubby, and she agreed to send me copies of the articles her library kept on file about them. No doubt she has fulfilled similar requests countless times, but such is the duty and service that stands behind her profession. (Hooray for librarians!)

One story in Patricia's packet changed the Stubby game for me. She included a 1998 article from the *Hartford Courant* that promoted the loaned display of the stuffed Stubby to the state armory museum. This much I had known already. But the article included a quote near the end from one Curtis Deane, speaking with great interest about Stubby because—drum roll, please—Robert Conroy was Curt's grandfather. Finally! A human connection to the human element of the story. It was the break I'd been looking for.

What followed was a lively e-mail correspondence combined with phone conversations and in-person visits, including a Smithsonian Stubby tour that we shared with other family members. It's always a pleasure to find someone who shares your research passion, and Curt and I swapped anecdotes and facts tirelessly. In addition to introducing me to other Conroy descendants, Curt provided invaluable help with the family's genealogy, adding flesh and heart to the story of a soldier and his dog.

Meanwhile, I pursued the broader trail, too. I studied the history of the Yankee Division, sought photographic evidence of its presence on the campus of Yale and in Europe, and pieced together the chronology of wartime events. By then I had already consumed Stubby's scrapbook, a cipher of disordered pages and unattributed clippings interspersed with charming but random artifacts. Here a train ticket. There a photograph (uncaptioned, as often as not). And page after page of newspaper articles, carefully clipped to preserve every word related to Stubby and, with horrifying consistency, maddeningly shorn of all details of provenance. When did the story appear? No idea. Where was it published? No clue. Patricia Watson and every other librarian—not to mention historian—would have been appalled.

Painstakingly, I began searching online databases to find replicas of the stories. Over time they began to emerge, dates and all, in such newspapers as the *New York Times*, the *Washington Post*, and the *Hartford Courant*.

Then the question became: How to make sense of them? Most of the stories repeated conflicting versions of the same "facts," seemingly copied by one reporter from another. For lack of a better strategy, I read every clipping and took notes on every mention of a "fact." Then I organized these note cards by topic and reconciled all the various accounts. Occasionally I would find a story, usually from a Connecticut paper, that quoted Conroy directly or that clearly had drawn on a direct interview with him. These pieces might as well have been printed on leaves of gold. I valued them over all other sources and filtered the body of research through the material that seemed closest to Conroy's voice.

After I met Curt, he was able to supply a brief but crucial document that confirmed my research method had been sound. His grandfather had prepared a two-page, legal-size account of Stubby, single-spaced, that summarized the dog's history, almost as if viewed from the point of view of the dog. No matter. The facts were there, even if Conroy had translated them into Stubby's vision. (For example, "Stubby decided to enlist in the Army, or perhaps Stubby heard of the fabulous Foreign Legion of France, an outfit in which one's past was never questioned.")

To create the wider context for the war I consulted scholarly accounts, such as Edward G. Lengel's *To Conquer Hell*, and primary source documents about the 26th Division. I read widely about dogs and dog history, too, all gauged to help me better understand the marvel of Stubby's story and the bonds that form between people and animals, especially during wartime.

Acknowledgments

I owe a special thanks to staff members at the Smithsonian Institution's National Museum of American History, especially Kathy Golden, who shared her collections with me on multiple occasions, including one visit I made with a group of Robert Conroy's descendants. She and her colleague Kay Peterson collaborated with me on the reproduction of many of the images found in Stubby's scrapbook, too.

My thanks go, as well, to historian Edward G. Lengel for his scholarship and his careful review of this book during production; to Patricia Watson and Oneil Cormier, Jr., at the New Britain Public Library; to Everett G. Shepherd of the Connecticut American Legion; to Edward Kasey, curator, and Frederick G. Horn, tour leader, for the West Haven Veterans Museum and Learning Center; and to staff members at Yale University's archives, Georgetown University, the Connecticut State Library, and the U.S. Army Military History Institute of Carlisle, Pennsylvania. I am particularly grateful to the Deane family for sharing their memories and, especially, to Curtis Deane for his many contributions during my research process, his review of my manuscript during production, and his authorship of the book's foreword.

Most of all, to Stubby and Robert Conroy: Thank you for living this story and making history along the way.

Bibliography

"102d Mascot Made Life Member of Y.M.C.A." *Hartford Courant*, May 9, 1919, 12.

"Body of Stubby, 26th Division Dog, Will Be on View." *Hartford Courant*, August 21, 1926, 11.

Cohan, George M. "Over There." New York: Leo Feist, Inc., 1917.

"Col. J. H. Parker Commands 102d." *Hartford Courant*, February 20, 1918, 5.

"Connecticut at Kansas City." *New Britain Herald*, 1921, editorial.*

Conroy, J. Robert. "Stubby A.E.F. Mascot." Scrapbook compiled and annotated by Conroy, held by Smithsonian Institution, National Museum of American History, Washington, D.C.

———. "Stubby, the Story of a Dog Who Made Himself Famous." Unpublished essay.

———. "'Stubby' Dog Mascot of Yankee Division Mourned by Soldiers." Obituary published 1926, unspecified media.

"Crowds Throng to Dog Show." *Boston Traveler*, February 25, 1920.

Daly, John J. "Sergeant Major Jiggs." *Washington Post*, January 16, 1927, SM: 1.

Deane, Curtis. Interviews conducted by Ann Bausum, February 11, 2013; March 9, 2013; April 2, 2013; May 4, 2013.

Derr, Mark. *A Dog's History of America*. New York, New York: North Point Press, 2004.

"A Dog of War." *Chicago Tribune*, October 30, 1921, 4.

"Dog Parade to Open 'Mutt' Show Today." *Washington Post*, November 20, 1925, 2.

"Edwards at Yankee Division Reunion." *New York Times*, July 4, 1921.

"Ex-Service Men United With Comrades Again at Christmas Dinner." *Hartford Courant*, December 26, 1922, 1, 2.

"The Faithful Dog." *Washington Post*, September 11, 1925, editorial: 6.

Fogle, Bruce. *Dog: The Definitive Guide for Dog Owners*. Buffalo, New York: Firefly Books, 2010.

"General Edwards at Reunion Today." *Hartford Courant*, August 28, 1920, 2.

"Gen. Edwards 'Idol of Outfit,' Says Conn. Governor." *Hartford Courant*, April 8, 1919, 6.

"General Pershing Decorates A.E.F. Dog Hero." *Army and Navy Journal*, undated.*

"'Got Two Germans Before They Got Me'—Plumridge." *Hartford Courant*, August 20, 1918, 3.

"Greatest of War Dogs to Attend Big Game." *Washington Post*, November 1, 1924, S1.

"'Happyland'—Even the Dog Wears the Smile That Means 'We're Home Again.'" *Boston American*, April 10, 1919, 3.

"Harding Applauds Animal Parade." *Washington Post*, May 14, 1921, 4.

"Here Are Three Fellow Warriors." *Sunday News* (Omaha, Nebraska), October 25, 1925.

"Hero Dog Hotel Guest." *New York Times*, December 31, 1922.

"James Conroy and His War Hero Dog in City." *Daily Press* (Newport News, Virginia), June 19, 1923, 9.

Kelley, Ralph J. "Stubby, the Canine Hero of the A.E.F." *Washington Post*, November 15, 1925, SM: 1, 5.

Kinghorn, Jonathan. *The Atlantic Transport Line, 1881–1931*. Jefferson, North Carolina: McFarland and Company, Inc., 2012.

"Last of Stubby, a Dog Hero." *New Britain Herald*, March 18, 1926, 6.

Lemish, Michael G. *War Dogs: A History of Loyalty and Heroism*. Washington, D.C.: Potomac Books, 2008.

Lengel, Edward G. *To Conquer Hell: The Meuse-Argonne, 1918, the Epic Battle That Ended the First World War*. New York: Henry Holt and Company, 2008.

"'The Lucky Dog.'" *Boston Traveler*, April 26, 1919.

Manning, George H. "Fenn Presents 'Stubby' Plaque." *New Britain Herald*, December 7, 1927.*

"Mascot of Army to Arrive Today." *Times-Picayune* (New Orleans), October 15, 1922.

"Mascots as Popular Today as They Were Centuries Ago." *New York Times*, April 17, 1927.

"Mascots Include Dog and a Goat." *Hartford Courant*, April 8, 1919, 1, 11.

"Most Decorated Dog in A.E.F." *Jacksonville Courier* (Jacksonville, Illinois), May 19, 1921, 1.

Nicholson, Tim, and Philomena Rutherford. *The Reader's Digest Illustrated Book of Dogs*, 2nd rev. ed. Pleasantville, New York: Reader's Digest Association, Inc., 1993.

"Now a Y.M.C.A. Life Member." *Hartford Courant*, May 11, 1919, 10.

Orlean, Susan. *Rin Tin Tin: The Life and the Legend*. New York: Simon & Schuster, 2011.

Owens, David. "A War Hero Stands Out." *Hartford Courant*, February 9, 1998.

"Pershing Honors Dog Hero." *Evening Bulletin* (Philadelphia, Pennsylvania), July 7, 1921.

"Pershing Honors Dog Mascot of A.E.F." *New York Times*, July 7, 1921, 1.

Photographic Supplement to Historical Record of Quartermaster Corps Activities A.E.F., Combat Troops at the Front. Tech. Rept. No. 2843-V8. Library of Congress, Prints and Photographs Collection, LOT 8330.

"Portrait of Stubby, Dog War Hero, Found." *New York Times*, January 18, 1931.

Richardson, Richard L. "A Crack at Stubby." *Stars and Stripes* (Washington, D.C.), August 27, 1921, letters to the editor: 5.

"Seicheprey Anniversary on Saturday." *Hartford Courant*, April 16, 1928, 14.

"Seicheprey YD War Hero." Connecticut Department, Veterans of Foreign Wars, April 1926.

"Semper Fido." *Washington Post*, November 14, 1993, Style: F1, F4, F5.

Service Records, Connecticut: Men and Women in the Armed Forces of the United States During World War, 1917-1920. Vols. 1 & 2. Hartford, Connecticut: Office of the Adjutant General, State Armory, publication undated.

"'Smiling Regiment,' Parker Calls 102d." *Hartford Courant*, March 12, 1918, 5.

Smith, Abbe. "'Stubby' the Dog Recalled for WWI Heroism." *New Haven Register*, November 12, 2009.

"State Comes to Hartford to Take Soldier Sons to Her Arms Again." *Hartford Courant*, May 1, 1919, 1, 10, 11.

"Stubby, 102d Mascot, Gets Third War Medal Decoration." *Hartford Courant*, July 8, 1921, 15.

"'Stubby,' 102d Mascot, to Be Guest at Christmas Dinner." *Hartford Courant*, December 13, 1922, 24.

"Stubby Decorated for Heroism by Pershing." *Washington Star*, July 7, 1921.

"'Stubby' Dies; Dog Gained Fame in War." *Washington Post*, March 17, 1926, 24.

"'Stubby' Dog Hero in Parade Today." *Washington Post*, May 11, 1921, 16.

"Stubby, Dog Hero, Is Honored Again." *Washington Post*, July 7, 1921, 14.

"'Stubby,' Famous War Dog, Becomes Full-Fledged Member of Eddy-Glover Post of American Legion," *New Britain Herald*, undated.*

"Stubby, Famous War Dog, Dies; Saw Action with 102d Regiment in France; Decorated by Pershing." *New Britain Herald*, March 17, 1926, 1, 15.

"'Stubby' Has Hiked With His Pals on Every Legion Parade Route." *Minneapolis Morning Tribune*, September 17, 1924.

"'Stubby,' Hero Dog, Is Awarded Medal at Show." *New Britain Herald*, February 24, 1920.

"'Stubby,' Heroic Mascot of 102d Infantry, Dies in Washington Home." *Hartford Courant*, March 18, 1926, 2.

"Stubby's History of Epic Warfare." *New Britain Herald*, March 24, 1926.

"'Stubby' Honored by General Pershing." *New Britain Herald*, July 7, 1921.

"Stubby, Legion Mascot, Here." *Kansas City Star*, October 1921.*

"'Stubby,' Most Decorated Dog, Meets Buddies in Omaha." *Evening Bee* (Omaha, Nebraska), October 8, 1925.

"Stubby of the A.E.F. Enters Valhalla." *New York Times*, April 4,1926.

"'Stubby,' of the Yankee Division." *Hartford Courant*, April 13, 1919, 19.

"Stubby, War Dog Hero, Will Be C.U. Mascot in State Game." *Washington Post*, November 1, 1920, 12.

"'Stubby," War Mascot, Honored by Comrades." *Washington Post*, December 5, 1927, 2.

"'Stubby' Will Have Tablet to Memory." *Hartford Courant*, November 30, 1927, 6.

"'Stubby,' YD Canine Hero, Dead." *New Haven Journal Courier*, 1926.

"'Stubby,' YD Mascot, Wins More Honors." *Hartford Courant*, February 25, 1920, 4.

"'Stubby,' Yankee Division Mascot, Returns to Honor Human Buddies." *New Britain Herald*, December 26, 1922.

Swager, Peggy. *Boston Terrier.* Freehold, New Jersey: Kennel Club Books, Inc., 2011.

"Tablet Commemorating Deeds of Stubby Given to Red Cross by Fenn." *Hartford Courant*, December 8, 1927, 9.

"Tells of Regard for Gen. Edwards." *Hartford Courant*, March 14, 1919.

Tucker, Ray T. "Ovation Without Parallel for New England's Own in Boston; 102d Wins Honors of Parade." *Hartford Courant*, April 26, 1919, 1, 2.

U.S. Congress, Senate *Congressional Record,* 101st Cong., 2d sess., S4823–24 (daily ed.), comments by George G. Vest.

"Veterans of Yankee Division Will Meet." *Washington Post*, December 14, 1924, 27.

Vickrey, Bab. "Three Canine War Heroes Enjoying Peace in Connecticut After Thrilling Trials Under Fire Along Western Front." *Bridgeport Herald*, August 8, 1920.

Whitehead, Sarah. *Dog: The Complete Guide.* New York: Barnes and Noble Books, 1999.

"Works for a Bonus (and a Bone)." *New York American*, June 5, 1923, 9.

"Wounded Dog Calls on Former Buddies." *Middleton Evening Press*, July 23, 1921, 10.

Wyatt, Franklin P. "A Known Warrior." (Unidentified source), 1921, letters to the editor.*

"YD Dog Given Medal." *Boston Traveler*, July 7, 1921.

* Publication information for some material taken from J. Robert Conroy's scrapbook could not be confirmed.

Resource Guide

Books of General Interest

Lemish, Michael G. *War Dogs: A History of Loyalty and Heroism.* Dulles, Virginia: Potomac Books, 2008.

Lengel, Edward G. *To Conquer Hell: The Meuse-Argonne, 1918.* New York: Henry Holt and Company, 2008.

Orlean, Susan. *Rin Tin Tin: The Life and the Legend.* New York: Simon & Schuster, 2011.

Books for Young Readers

Freedman, Russell. *The War to End All Wars: World War I.* New York: Clarion Books, 2010.

Kennedy, Patricia Burlin. *Through Otis' Eyes: Lessons from a Guide Dog Puppy.* New York: Howell Book House, 1998.

Murphy, Jim. *Truce: The Day the Soldiers Stopped Fighting.* New York: Scholastic Press, 2009.

Patent, Dorothy Hinshaw. *Dogs on Duty: Soldiers' Best Friends on the Battlefield and Beyond.* New York: Walker & Company, 2012.

Music

Historic American Sheet Music, online database

"Over There" and other songs from World War I

Library of Congress and Duke University

memory.loc.gov/ammem/award97/ncdhtml/hasmhome.html

Documentary Film

The Complete Story: World War I
A BBC/CBS production from 1964. Reissued by Timeless Media Group, 2005.

Places to Visit in Person and Online

First Division Museum at Cantigny

1s151 Winfield Road
Wheaton, IL 60189

630-260-8185

firstdivisionmuseum.org

National World War I Museum

100 West 26th Street
Kansas City, MO 64108

816-888-8100

theworldwar.org

"The Price of Freedom: Americans at War"

National Museum of American History

Smithsonian Institution
1400 Constitution Avenue, N.W.
Washington, DC 20001

202-633-1000

amhistory.si.edu/militaryhistory

Smithsonian Institution

National Museum of American History

Contains Stubby's object record

amhistory.si.edu/militaryhistory/collection/object.asp?ID=15&back=1

West Haven Veterans Museum

Honors the 26th Division and other Connecticut service members

30 Hood Terrace
West Haven, CT 06516

203-934-1111

whmilmuseum.com

Citations

Front Matter

PHOTO CAPTIONS: p. 5, J. Robert Conroy: "perhaps the only American dog…and return home." (Conroy, "'Stubby' Dog Mascot of Yankee Division Mourned by Soldiers").

❶ A Dog's Best Friend

RAISED QUOTE: p. 10, George G. Vest: "The one absolutely unselfish friend…is his dog." (U.S. Congress, Senate *Congressional Record*, 101st Cong., 2d sess., pp. S4823-24 daily ed.).

TEXT: p. 14, J. Robert Conroy: Stubby "completed his boot training" and "full-fledged mascot." (Conroy, "Stubby, The Story of a Dog Who Made Himself Famous"); p. 17, Conroy: "Stubby was sadly told…could not understand that." (Conroy: "Stubby, The Story of a Dog Who Made Himself Famous").

❷ Over There

RAISED QUOTES: p. 18, Excerpted lyrics from "Over There" (George M. Cohan, 1917, Leo Feist, Inc.); p. 27, J. Robert Conroy: "It seemed…never wavered." (Conroy, "'Stubby,' Dog Mascot of Yankee Division Mourned by Soldiers").

TEXT: p. 19, J. Robert Conroy: "good interference." (Conroy: "Stubby, The Story of a Dog Who Made Himself Famous"); p. 20, Edward G. Lengel, "would do anything for him." (Lengel: p. 362); p. 21, published news story: "Stubby was the only member…and get away with it." ("Stubby, Famous War Dog, Dies"); p. 22, Conroy: "Stubby was always on his own…expected to remain a live mascot." (Conroy: "Stubby, The Story of a Dog Who Made Himself Famous"); p. 22, Conroy: "closest comrade…during the war." (Conroy, "'Stubby,' Dog Mascot of Yankee Division Mourned by Soldiers"); p. 25, newspaper article: "never yelped." ("'Stubby,' of the Yankee Division"); p. 25, Sgt. John J. Curtin, poem: "He always knew…first gas smells." (Conroy, "Stubby A.E.F. Mascot": scrapbook p. 34, undated manuscript); p. 26, supply record: "potatoes, onions…and cabbages." (Photographic Supplement to Historical Record of Quartermaster Corps Activities A.E.F., Combat Troops at the Front: p. 49); p. 26, soldier in the 102nd: "big round loaves…welcome to a hungry man." ("'Smiling Regiment,' Parker Calls 102nd").

❸ In the Trenches

RAISED QUOTES: p. 28, Lt. Ralph Kynoch: "If we can't get a dog…give us a DOG first." (Conroy, "Stubby A.E.F. Mascot": scrapbook p. 37, unattributed clipping entitled "Dogs and the Soldier"); p. 36, editorial: "There are times when…attributes of a human being." ("Last of Stubby, A Dog Hero").

PHOTO CAPTIONS: p. 32, photographer: "Their 'cooties' are gone…small boys from a school picnic." (Photographic Supplement to Historical Record of Quartermaster Corps Activities A.E.F., Combat Troops at the Front: p. 78).

TEXT: p. 29, newspaper article: "For days…Stubby should not get well." ("Wounded Dog Calls on Former Buddies"); p. 29, J. Robert Conroy: "was like the proverbial cat…have many lives." (Conroy, "Stubby, The Story of a Dog Who Made Himself Famous"); p. 34, photographer: "Note the happy appearance…about to leave." (Photographic Supplement to Historical Record of Quartermaster Corps Activities A.E.F., Combat Troops at the Front: p. 69); p. 38, news report: "gallantry." ("Veterans of Yankee Division Will Meet"); p. 38, service records: "wounded in action slightly." (Service Records, Connecticut, Vol. 2, p. 1513); p. 38, Capt. Bob Casey: "The silence is oppressive. It weighs in on one's eardrums." (Lengel, p. 408); p. 38, news report: "Hundreds of friends…the good luck of victory." (Conroy, "Stubby A.E.F. Mascot": scrapbook p. 27, *New Britain Herald*, undated editorial).

❹ Victory Lap

RAISED QUOTE: p. 40, Sgt. John J. Curtin, poem: "He is a fighting bulldog…night and day." (Conroy, "Stubby A.E.F. Mascot": scrapbook p. 34, undated manuscript).

TEXT: p. 43, J. Robert Conroy: "a regulation barred… convalescing soldier." (Conroy: "Stubby, The Story of a Dog Who Made Himself Famous"); p. 44, causes of death, "suicide" (Service Records, Connecticut, Vol. I, p. 233), "vessel was torpedoed and sunk" (Service Records, Connecticut, Vol. 2, p. 1622), "accidental drowning" (Service Records, Connecticut, Vol. 2, p. 1573); p. 47, news report: "the most famous dog in the American army." (Conroy, "Stubby A.E.F. Mascot": scrapbook p. 51, unattributed clipping fragment); p. 47, Mrs. O'Brien: "Nobody could mind Stubby…They are regular chums." (Vickrey); p. 47, Boston dog show judge: "He's probably a mutt…all the rest put together." (Vickrey).

❺ At Ease, Sgt. Stubby

RAISED QUOTES: p. 48, Warren G. Harding: "Whether the Creator planned it…a brave and devoted dog." (Kelley); p. 54, "Stubby only a dog?…the great spirit that hovered over the 26th." ("Last of Stubby, a Dog Hero").

TEXT: p. 50, news report: "bravery under fire." (Conroy, "Stubby A.E.F. Mascot": scrapbook p. 26, unattributed clipping entitled "'Twas 'Stubby's' Day"); p. 50, J. Robert Conroy: "At the entrance…the bar was removed." (Conroy: "Stubby, The Story of a Dog Who Made Himself Famous"); p. 50, Conroy, scrapbook entry: "Mrs. Harding held Stubby's leash for ten minutes." (Conroy, "Stubby A.E.F. Mascot": scrapbook p. 64, handwritten note); p. 50, *New York Times*: "In the World War part of a leg was shot off." ("Mascots as Popular Today as They Were Centuries Ago"); p. 50, news report: "Stuffy," "toughy," "he happened to stop five bullets." (Conroy, "Stubby A.E.F. Mascot": scrapbook p. 57, unattributed clipping entitled "'Stuffy,' Real War Dog, Is Booked for Exhibition Here"); p. 53, Franklin P. Wyatt: "ex-soldiers are starving in the streets of our big cities." (Conroy, "Stubby A.E.F. Mascot": scrapbook p. 15, undated letter to the editor entitled "A Known Warrior"); p. 53, Richard L. Richardson: "If this Boston bull did so much…the next time?" (Richardson); p. 53, Conroy: "Criticism of Stubby which proves he is famous." (Conroy, "Stubby A.E.F. Mascot": scrapbook p. 15, handwritten note); p. 53, Conroy: "One day when Stubby was near…a minor operation for Stubby." (Conroy, "Stubby, The Story of a Dog Who Made Himself Famous"); p. 54, news account: "looked around, apparently bewildered…in a perfect canine salute." ("Stubby, YD Mascot, Returns to Honor Human Buddies"); p. 54, Conroy: "Stubby's seal." ("'Stubby,' Famous War Dog, Becomes Full-Fledged Member of Eddy-Glover Post of American Legion"); p. 55, "Machine Gun" Parker: "He will be mourned…of our comrades." (Conroy, "Stubby, The Story of a Dog Who Made Himself Famous"); p. 55, Conroy: "All who knew him…and been kind to him." (Conroy, "'Stubby' Dog Mascot of Yankee Division Mourned by Soldiers").

Afterword

RAISED QUOTE: p. 56, editorial: "The boys loved him…is snapped." ("'Stubby,' YD Canine Hero, Dead").

TEXT: p. 57, Curtis Deane: "My grandfather always said Stubby adopted him." (Deane: interview, February 11, 2013); p. 57, Deane: "was always very quiet…got him through the war." (Deane: interview, March 9, 2013); p. 57, Deane: "Stubby was his avocation." (Deane: interview, March 9, 2013); p. 59, Deane: "He was very proud of Stubby." (Deane: interview, March 9, 2013); p. 60, Deane: "a gentleman 20 ways to Sunday." (Deane: interview, February 11, 2013); p. 60–61, Deane: "He was a proud man with a lot of dignity." (Deane: interview, February 11, 2013); p. 61, Deane's account of Conroy's death: "Margaret, I love you very much, but I've had enough." And "he closed his eyes and died." (Deane: interview, February 11, 2013).

Time Line

TEXT: p. 63, YMCA membership card: "good for three bones a day" and "a place to sleep." (Conroy, "Stubby A.E.F. Mascot": scrapbook p. 42, artifact).

Research Notes

TEXT: p. 65, Conroy: "Stubby decided…was never questioned." (Conroy, "Stubby, The Story of a Dog Who Made Himself Famous").

Index

Boldface indicates illustrations.

A

Agamemnon (ship) 43

Allied Powers 13, 25, 42

C

Central Powers 13

Château-Thierry, France 34, 42, 53

Chemin des Dames, France 22

Cher Ami (carrier pigeon) 57

Conroy, J. Robert
artifacts in Smithsonian Institution 57–58

bond with Stubby 12, 22, 30, 57

death 60–61

family 12, 47, **52, 58**

Georgetown University law school 49, 53

life after Stubby 59, 60

military discharge 47

in Paris 34–35

postwar duties 41

promotions 26, 38

in Seicheprey, France 26–27

sense of humor 17, 43, 50

shipping out to Europe 17, 19

souvenirs **45**

Spanish flu 38, 42–43

with Stubby **4, 7, 10, 31, 59, 62**

Stubby's American Legion membership 54

Stubby's death 54–55

Stubby's scrapbook 30, **34–35**, 53, 58

Stubby's shrapnel injury 27, 29

vaudeville shows 47

volunteering for World War I service 13–14

work on Capitol Hill 53–54, **59**

wounded by poisonous gas 38

Yankee Division duties 20, 22, 30

Coolidge, Calvin 44, 50, **52**

Cooties (lice) 26, 32, 33–34, 44

Curtin, John J. 25

D

Deane, Curtis 6–7, 57, **58,** 59, 60–61

Dogs
military service 22, 41, 59

postwar treatment 41, 44

Doughboys
battle keepsakes 38

definition 14

diversity 14, **15**

food 26

funk holes (underground bunkers) **27**

military training 14, **15, 16**

recruitment **15, 18,** 19

Duncan, Lee 44

E

Edwards, Clarence 20, 38, 44

F

Forty and eight boxcars **16, 17**

France
canine service dogs 41

children watching 101st Infantry **20–21**

forty and eight boxcars **16, 17**

Funk holes (underground bunkers) **27**

G

Gas, poisonous **23,** 25, 29

Gas masks **23,** 25, **29**

Georgetown University 49–50, 53

German army 25, 33, **37, 62**

Goats 30, 33, 43–44, **45**

H

Harding, Warren G. 50, **51,** 52

Humane Education Society 50

L

Laddie boy (dog) 50, **51**

Lengel, Edward G. 20, 44

Lice 26, 32, 33–34, 44

M

Mademoiselle Fanny (goat) 30, 33, 43–44, **45**

Mascots 30, 43–44

Meuse-Argonne campaign 35–37, 38

Minnesota (ship) 17, 19, **19**

P

Parker, John Henry "Machine Gun" 21, 26, 55

Pershing, John J. **41,** 50, **51**

Pickelhaube (spiked helmet) **37**

Poisonous gas **23,** 25, 29

Prisoners of war 33, 35

R

Rags (dog) **31**

Railroad gun **24**

Rats 26

Rin Tin Tin (dog) 44

S

Seicheprey, France 26–27

Sergeant Major Jiggs (dog) **51**

Service dogs 59

Simpson, Edward 30, 43–44

Smithsonian Institution, Washington, D.C. 57

St. Mihiel, France 35, 41

Stubby
adopted by French soldier 22

aging 54

American Legion 53, 54

appearance 11

bond with Conroy 12, 22, 30, 57

in combat 22, 25, 26–27

with Conroy **4, 7, 10, 31, 59, 62**

with Conroy's family 47, **52**

Conroy's scrapbook 30, **34–35**, 53, 58

Conroy's Spanish flu hospitalization 43

death 54–55, 57

duties 20, 26, 30, 33

fame **49,** 49–53, **61**

gas attacks 25, 38

gas mask 23, 25

as Georgetown University mascot **48,** 49–50, 53

Hero Dog award 47

heroism 25, 35

medals 38, 41–42, **42, 43,** 50, **51, 60**

meeting Presidents 41, 50, **52**

as military mascot 14, 20, 21, 22, 41

military rank 37–38

military training 14

in parades 44, **46,** 47, 50, **57**

in Paris 34–35

portrait **55, 61, 63**

prisoners of war 33, 35, 37

return home from France 43

saluting 14, 19–20, 54

shipping out to Europe 17, 19

shrapnel injury 27, 29

in Smithsonian Institution **56,** 57, 58, 59–60

uniform 34, **34, 42, 43, 60**

vaudeville 46, 47, **63**

at Washington Monument 53

at Yale University 11–12

T

Tanks **23**

Time line 62–63

Trench warfare 13, **28**

V

Vaudeville shows 46, 47

Verdun, France **36,** 41

W

Washington Monument, Washington, D.C. 53

Wilson, Woodrow 41

World War I **62**
   end of war celebrations 38–39, **40, 41, 49**
   food for soldiers 26
   medical staff 27, 29, **39**
   military technology 13
   opposing forces 12–13
   outbreak 12
   trench warfare 13, **28**
   weapons 13, **24,** 25

Y

Yale University **11,** 11–12

Yankee Division **13, 31**
   on front lines 22
   marching in France **20–21**
   Meuse-Argonne campaign 35–37
   nickname 20
   victory parade 44, 47

Illustrations Credits

Except where noted below, illustrations are reproduced from Stubby's scrapbook, courtesy Armed Forces History, Smithsonian Institution. Illustrations credits preceded by the initials LC are reproduced courtesy the Library of Congress Prints & Photographs Division. Items marked AB came from the author's collections. Illustrations marked NGS were provided by the National Geographic Society. All textured background panels are courtesy Shutterstock.

Background image on front cover and pp. 2-3, Getty Images/Hulton Archives 3276578; pp. 4-5, background image, LC-DIG-ds-04300; p. 9, AB; p. 11, Yale University Military and Wartime Activities Photographs (collection RU 750), Manuscripts and Archives, Yale University Library; pp. 12-13, LC, PAN US MILITARY-Army no. 115; p. 15, upper, LC-DIG-ds-04289; p. 15, lower left, LC-USZC4-9662; p. 15, lower right, LC-USZ62-116442; p. 16, upper, LC-DIG-ds-04293; p. 16, lower right, LC-USZ62-49030; p. 17, LC-DIG-ds-04288; p. 18, LC-USZC4-9875; p. 19, Langhorne Gibson Papers, Manuscripts and Archives, Yale University Library; pp. 20-21, LC-USZ62-98381; p. 23, upper, LC-USZ62-115014; p. 23, lower, LC-USZ62-64469; p. 24, upper, LC-DIG-ds-04290; p. 24, lower, LC-USZ62-64471; p. 27, LC-DIG-ds-04287; p. 28, LC-USZ62-41941; p. 29, LC-USZ62-42731; p. 31, lower right, Bettman/CORBIS; p. 32, upper, LC-DIG-ds-04299; p. 32, middle, LC-DIG-ds-04291; p. 32, lower, LC-DIG-ds-04298; p. 37, LC-USZ62-136092; p. 39, LC-USZ62-37482; p. 40, LC-USZ62-36567; p. 41, LC-USZ62-36561; p. 42, left, AB; p. 42, right, AB/NGS; p. 43, Bettman/CORBIS U264080INP; p. 45, lower right, AB/NGS; p. 51, lower left, LC-DIG-npcc-13411; p. 51, lower right, LC-USZ62-65037; p. 52, middle, LC-USZ62-58102; p. 56, Lori Epstein, NGS; p. 57, Bettman/CORBIS; p. 58, courtesy of Curtis Deane; p. 60, courtesy West Haven Veterans Museum and Learning Center; p. 61, AB/NGS; p. 62, lower, LC-USZ62-136100; p. 63, right, AB, courtesy West Haven Veterans Museum and Learning Center; p. 68, "Over There," Music 1170, Historic American Sheet Music Project, David M. Rubenstein Rare Book & Manuscript Library, Duke University; trade case, Terry Waldron-Tottenham/ www.terryjamesart.com.

Prepared by the Book Division

Hector Sierra, *Senior Vice President and General Manager*

Nancy Laties Feresten, *Senior Vice President, Kids Publishing and Media*

Jennifer Emmett, *Vice President, Editorial Director, Children's Books*

Eva Absher-Schantz, *Design Director, Kids Publishing and Media*

Jay Sumner, *Director of Photography, Children's Publishing*

R. Gary Colbert, *Production Director*

Jennifer A. Thornton, *Director of Managing Editorial*

Staff for This Book

Jennifer Emmett, *Project Editor*

David Seager, *Art Director*

Lori Epstein, *Senior Photo Editor*

Marty Ittner, *Designer*

Ariane Szu-Tu, *Editorial Assistant*

Callie Broaddus, *Design Production Assistant*

Margaret Leist, *Photo Assistant*

Grace Hill, *Associate Managing Editor*

Joan Gossett, Michael O'Connor, *Production Editors*

Lewis R. Bassford, *Production Manager*

Susan Borke, *Legal and Business Affairs*

Cathleen Carey and Moriah Petty, *Interns*

Production Services

Phillip L. Schlosser, *Senior Vice President*

Chris Brown, *Vice President, NG Book Manufacturing*

Rachel Faulise, *Manager*

Haley Harrington, *Imaging Technician*

Since 1888, the National Geographic Society has funded more than 12,000 research, exploration, and preservation projects around the world. The Society receives funds from National Geographic Partners, LLC, funded in part by your purchase. A portion of the proceeds from this book supports this vital work. To learn more, visit natgeo.com/info.

NATIONAL GEOGRAPHIC and Yellow Border Design are trademarks of the National Geographic Society, used under license.

For more information, please visit nationalgeographic.com, call 1-800-647-5463, or write to the following address:

National Geographic Partners
1145 17th Street N.W.
Washington, D.C. 20036-4688 U.S.A.

Visit us online at nationalgeographic.com/books

For librarians and teachers: ngchildrensbooks.org

More for kids from National Geographic: natgeokids.com

For information about special discounts for bulk purchases, please contact National Geographic Books Special Sales: specialsales@natgeo.com

For rights or permissions inquiries, please contact National Geographic Books Subsidiary Rights: bookrights@natgeo.com

Hardcover ISBN: 978-1-4263-1486-5
Reinforced library edition ISBN: 978-1-4263-1487-2
Paperback ISBN: 978-1-4263-3266-1

A Note on the Design

The design inspiration for *Stubby the War Dog* is twofold. Partly, the image and design elements are based on World War I posters and military motifs. The design pages, in particular the ones on green backgrounds, also evoke Stubby's own scrapbook. J. Robert Conroy, Stubby's friend and owner, gathered Stubby's clippings, awards, and souvenir items into a single volume of memories. The scrapbook, along with Stubby's signature medal coat—and Stubby himself!—are now part of the collection of the Smithsonian Institution.

The text for the book is set in Avenir, Rockwell, and Farao.

National Geographic supports K–12 educators with ELA Common Core Resources. Visit www.natgeoed.org/commoncore for more information.

Printed in China
18/PPS/1